Visiting Hour

A play

Richard Harris

Samuel French - London
New York - Toronto - Hollywood

VISITING HOUR

First presented as a National Theatre Platform performance in the Cottesloe Theatre on 30th September 1987,
with the following cast:

Eric	Russell Dixon
Helen	Marcia Warren
Pauline	Diane Bull
Old Woman	Marcia Warren
Brenda	Diane Bull
Ron	Russell Dixon
Joan	Marcia Warren
Nurses	Kate Dyson
	Tel Stevens

Directed by Michael Gambon
Designed by Soraya Walton
Produced by Amanda Saunders

The revised version of the play was first presented at The
Duke's Head Theatre, Richmond, Surrey, on 26th June
1990, with the following cast:

Eric	Colin Starkey
Helen	Marcia Warren
Pauline	Susan Jameson
Old Woman	Angela Rooks
Naomi	Susan Jameson
Fiona	Ganiat Kasumu
Darbon	Walter Sparrow
Nurse **Son-in-law** **Father** **Critic**	Colin Starkey
Maureen **Woman critic** **2nd Reader**	Marcia Warren

Julia
Daughter
Mother   Angela Rooks
Reader

Cheryl   Marcia Warren
Tricia   Ganiat Kasumu
Hazel   Angela Rooks
Eileen   Susan Jameson
Visitor   Walter Sparrow
Husband   Colin Starkey

Old Man   Walter Sparrow
Nurse   Ganiat Kasumu

May   Angela Rooks
Arthur   Walter Sparrow
Sandra   Ganiat Kasumu
Brenda   Susan Jameson
Ron   Colin Starkey
Joan   Marcia Warren

Directed by David Gillies
Produced by Sally Campbell

AUTHOR'S NOTE

Visiting Hour was written for a company of six actors, each to play several parts in the six scenes which make up the piece. However, I do not consider it obligatory that all six scenes should be played together, so that a company might make up their performance by choosing only some of the scenes, mixing the comic and the not-so-comic according to taste.

The non-speaking Nurses are played by members of the stage management—the more nursing staff to create hospital "atmosphere" between scenes, the better. You might very happily include the tea lady and her wayward trolley . . .

CHARACTERS

ACT I

PLASTER
Eric
Helen

KEEPING MUM
Pauline
Old Woman

SHOW BUSINESS
Naomi
Fiona
Darbon
Male Nurse ⎫
Son-in-law ⎪
Father ⎬ may be played by the same actor
Critic ⎭
Maureen ⎫
Woman Critic ⎬ may be played by the same actress
2nd Reader ⎭
Julia ⎫
Daughter ⎪
Mother ⎬ may be played by the same actress
Reader ⎭

ACT II

GOING HOME
Cheryl
Tricia
Hazel
Eileen
Visitor
Husband

WAITING
Old Man
Nurse

MAGIC
May
Arthur
Sandra
Brenda
Ron
Joan

The action takes place in a hospital ward

Time—the present

CONTENTS

*Published separately by Samuel French Ltd

Plays by Richard Harris
published by Samuel French Ltd

One Act:
Albert
Is It Something I Said?
Keeping Mum (*from* Visiting Hour)

Full Length:
The Business of Murder
Local Affairs
The Maintenance Man
Outside Edge
Partners
Stepping Out

Written with Leslie Darbon:
Two and Two Make Sex
Who Goes Bare?

ACT I

A hospital ward

There are three doors (or exits): DR, UR and UL, and three beds—one DR, and two upstage. Each bed has the usual bedside cabinet, visitors' chairs, temperature chart, etc., with a set of radio headphones and oxygen outlet above it. At the foot of the UL bed there is a bed-tray. There is a curtain rail in the ceiling so that each of the upstage beds may be curtained off

As the CURTAIN rises, the ward is in half-light. The UL bed is empty. The UR bed has the curtains closed. The DR bed contains the motionless body of an Old Woman. She lies on her side, away from us, so that all we see of her is her grey hair. But she should be so small and still that we scarcely notice that she is there

Plaster

A Nurse enters UR. As she does, the area around the curtained bed lights up and we hear the distorted jangle of hospital sounds: tannoy messages for doctors, ambulance sirens, patients calling for attention, etc. She crosses to pull back the curtains, revealing the bed, and straightaway exits L

A middle-aged man with a moustache is propped up by pillows on top of the bed. He is encased from head to foot in plaster and bandages. His legs are spread wide. One of his arms is in a sling. The forefinger of that hand has a sticking plaster on it. Only his head—which is encased in a bandage helmet—is mobile. His eyes are closed in sleep

The hospital noises fade and a handbell rings

After a moment, Helen—a middle-aged woman—enters R. She wears a topcoat and hat and carries a handbag and basket. She moves to the bed and looks down at him for a moment

Helen Eric?

No response. She puts down the basket and leans closer

    Eric?

Still nothing. She leans closer still

    Eric?

And suddenly his eyes open sharply, making her start, and he jerks upright with:

Eric I can explain everything, it's quite simple actually ... (*He realizes that*

he has come out of a bad dream. Resting back against the pillows) Who's
that?
Helen It's me, Eric—Helen.
Eric Oh.
Helen You were dreaming.
Eric Give me my glasses, will you?
Helen Where are they?
Eric I don't know—on the side there somewhere.

She sees them on top of the cabinet

Helen You're quite right, Eric—as per—here they are—sorry. (*She puts the
glasses on him. It isn't easy with his head encased in the helmet of bandages*)
Eric Careful, careful.
Helen There.

*He focuses. She smiles at him. He groans at seeing her. She turns the chair and
sits*

Well. You're looking better, I must say.
Eric How can I be looking better? Look at me.
Helen What I mean is, you've got a bit of colour in your cheeks.
Eric Oh well—if I've got a bit of colour in my cheeks, no doubt they'll be
discharging me tomorrow—I should hate to be occupying a bed unneces-
sarily.
Helen You haven't lost your sense of humour, then.
Eric No, Helen. I have lost the use of both arms, I have lost the use of both
legs. I have lost three back teeth, six pints of blood and very nearly the will
to live, but what I have not lost is my sense of humour, aren't I the lucky
one?

A moment

Helen Anyway. It's nice to have you back.
Eric Nice to what?
Helen Have you back. Out of your coma. Did they bring you round or did
you manage it all by yourself?
Eric It so happens I came out of my coma, uninduced, just before midnight.
And what do I find? (*He raises his head to look down at his body*) This lot.
Helen Yes, you're going to need a lot of looking after, Eric—and I know
who'll be expected to do it. I'll clean your glasses, shall I, they look a bit
grubby.

*And before he can protest, she stands and is taking off his glasses, none-too-
gently, and cleaning them with a handkerchief she takes from her bag as:*

Eric Have you been coming every day?
Helen Every day, yes.
Eric Just sitting here?
Helen Only yesterday. Before that, they'd only let me have a quick peek
through the window, you being critical. But he's always been critical, I
said, that's his way.

Eric Oh yes, Helen, very sharp, very witty.

She gets the glasses back on him, and sits

(*Closing his eyes*) Did you by any chance bring any titbits?

Helen No solids, she said—not for a day or two—so I bought you some nice soup and one of my trifles. Would you like a little something now?

Eric (*mock-patiently*) That would be very nice, Helen.

His eyes remain closed as she takes the tray from the foot of the bed and puts it across his legs, then takes a bowl and spoon from the basket and puts them on the tray as she speaks

Helen Can you remember anything about it?

Eric What?

Helen The accident.

Eric Not a lot—no.

Helen (*taking a Thermos flask from the basket*) That would be the shock, would it?

Eric Presumably.

She is trying to unscrew the top. From force of habit, she holds it out to him to do, then realizes that he is, of course, incapable. During the following, she will manage to get the lid off

Helen The policeman who came round said you were lucky to be alive.

Eric Did he.

Helen When you consider the circumstances, he said.

Eric (*eyes opening*) Circumstances?

Helen How it happened.

During the following, she will pour soup into the bowl and stand the flask on the cabinet and then take out a gingham tablecloth from the basket and tuck it into his bandages as a napkin

Eric I presume he didn't go into details.

Helen No, not really. He just said you'd been in a car accident. My stomach turned right over. But he's such a careful driver, I said. Ah yes, he said, but the car wasn't actually *moving*.

As they talk, she spoonfeeds him the soup—which is very hot—so that he reacts and she blows on the spoon

Eric But he didn't actually go into details.

Helen No. He didn't want to worry me, I suppose. (*Dabbing his mouth*) They found your book by the way. That's one thing you don't have to worry about. (*She continues feeding him*)

Eric What book?

Helen The little book you write your jokes in. He'll be so pleased, I said. They gave it to me with all your other personal possessions. You being next-of-kin, he said. (*A little shudder*) Ooo, it quite made me shudder.

Eric Standard procedure, Helen.

Helen Mind you, he was quite suspicious.

Eric Who was?

During the following, the spoonful of soup is poised near his open mouth and he makes unsuccessful attempts to get at it as Helen concentrates on her narrative

Helen The policeman. We found this book, he said. When they were cutting him out of the wreckage. Oh, that's his joke book, I said. His book of jokes. Oh yes? He said, how'd you mean? Well, I said, my husband is a sales executive and when he hears a good joke he writes it down so that he can tell his clients.

Eric Very good, Helen.

Helen Anyway, I put it straight into your bureau. (*She gives him the spoonful of soup and dabs his mouth*) With your wallet and so forth.

Eric Thank you.

Helen Not your glasses though. I brought those in yesterday. Knowing how lost you are without them.

Pause

That was one of the things he asked me, actually.

Eric Who?

Helen The policeman.

Eric How d'you mean—asked you?

Helen He'll be so pleased they're not broken, I said—he can't see a thing without his glasses. Does he use them for driving then, he said. Oh yes, I said, he uses them for everything. Oh, he said.

Slight pause

Eric Oh, he said, what?

Helen Oh, he said. We found them in their case in his coat pocket. Well he must have taken them off, I said. Only what for, I can't imagine. The only times he removes his glasses are when he goes to bed and during the odd moment of personal vanity. Photographs, for example.

Eric There was something in my eye.

Helen I thought that might be it—that would be why he stopped the car, I said.

Eric Correct.

Helen That's fate though, isn't it? You stop the car to get something out of your eye and the next thing you know, something's crashing into the back of you. What was it, a fly or something?

Eric No, it was a large lorry.

Helen There you go again, always joking. No, I mean in your eye.

Eric That's right, Helen. A fly.

Helen I expect it flew in through the window.

Eric No, no—it was hitch-hiking, I picked it up on the motorway. Helen, don't worry how it happened—it happened and that's all you need to know about. Don't tax your brain.

She resumes feeding him for a moment

Helen All gone. (*Returning the Thermos, bowl and spoon to the basket*) Only what he was trying to work out, this policeman, was how a fly could have come in through a window when all the windows were tightly-closed, which was quite strange in itself, really, it being such a warm evening.

His face contorts as he considers an answer

Eric I closed the windows . . . in order to keep the little buggers out. If you yourself drove you would know how distracting and, therefore, dangerous they can be. Unfortunately, I was too late.

Helen I said that would be it. Or something like that. Anyway. You can imagine what a shock it was when he knocked on the door and told me. My stomach turned right over. When did it happen, I said. About eight o'clock, he said. Oh, I say, I said, he only phoned me at seven to say he wouldn't be back until gone eleven. Oh, he *phoned*, he said. Oh yes, I said, he always phones me when he's going to be late home, he's very good like that, wherever he is he always manages to find a phone box. Oh yes. Without fail. Half his salary must go on tenpenny pieces telling me he'll be late home. (*Of the soup*) Was that nice?

Eric Delightful.

Helen Would you like some more or will you go straight on to the trifle?

Eric I'll have the trifle. In a moment.

She puts the basket on the floor. A moment. She nods pleasantly to an unseen patient who is passing

Helen What he couldn't understand was why you were in Potters Bar.

Eric What?

Helen Us living in Ealing and you being delayed coming from Bournemouth. Why you should go via Potters Bar.

Again the facial contortions from him

Eric Bournemouth? Who said anything about Bournemouth?

Helen You did. I'm with a client in Bournemouth you said. Don't wait up, I shall be delayed, you said.

Slight moment

Eric A client *called* Bournemouth. Mr Bournemouth. Mr Bournemouth of Potters Bar. Limited.

Helen reacts: of course *that's what he said*

Helen Not only stupid but going deaf: I don't know how you put up with me. Are you ready for your trifle? I can't do much, but I can make a good trifle, even *you* say that, Eric.

During the following, she takes a plastic box from the basket, removes the lid, and spoons out trifle on to a plate, then replaces the lid

I suppose we were lucky it didn't happen on a main road.

Eric What?

Helen The accident. It could have caused a multiple pile-up. Thank goodness you had the presence of mind to turn off the main road when

that fly got in your eye. Mind you, he's always been able to think fast, I
said. What's that expression you use——?

Eric —the ability to think on one's feet.

Helen Not like me, then, Eric.

Eric One can, as they say, only get so much out of a turnip.

*She delicately spoons trifle into his mouth and will continue to do so
throughout the following*

Helen Oh yes, that reminds me—in case you're wondering about your
trousers, they're at the cleaners.

He frowns, trying to work out what she means

Your trousers. The trousers to your suit.

Eric What about my trousers?

Helen You weren't wearing them. When they brought you into hospital.

Eric No ... well ... I—I wouldn't be, would I?

Helen He wasn't wearing his trousers, he said. The policeman. That's not
like Eric, I said—he's very fastidious about things like that—there must
be a reason, I mean he wouldn't just——

Eric Of course there's a reason. They couldn't get the door of the car open
so they had to get me through the window. In order to facilitate my exit, I
was asked by the chief fireman to remove some of my clothing.

Helen So you took off your trousers.

Eric Precisely.

Helen Anyway. He brought them round and they're at the cleaners. (*She
slips more trifle into his mouth*) Nice?

He chews, can't answer. She dabs his mouth

He's already made a statement, apparently.

Eric Who has?

Helen The lorry driver. He says it was a private lane used only by farm
traffic, and you were parked there in a particularly dark spot without any
lights on and him crashing into the back of you was entirely your own
fault.

Eric I switched off the lights in order to conserve the battery.

Helen You don't have to convince me, Eric. Some of these people. I don't
know. Any excuse to get out of trouble.

Eric I've no doubt we shall settle on a knock for knock basis.

Helen Anyway. He didn't have a witness. (*She spoons trifle into his mouth*)
Not like you, Eric. Fortunately, your husband had a witness, he said. The
policeman. He did tell me the name but typically it seems to have slipped
my mind. (*She dabs his mouth*)

Eric (*mumbling*) O'Connell.

Helen Sorry?

Eric O'Connell.

Helen That's right. O'Connell. Miss O'Connell.

He clears his throat

Eric Mrs.

Helen Mrs O'Connell. Yes. Presumably she's a business associate of your husband's, he said—she, like you, being in a coma apparently. I've no idea, Officer, I said, the name certainly doesn't——

Eric —Mrs O'Connell has only recently joined the sales force——

Helen That's why then. I knew there'd be a——

Eric —this is her first position on the sales side which naturally means that she required experience in the field.

Helen And you've been giving it to her.

Eric Quite.

She spoons trifle into his mouth and sits

Helen Now then. Let me see if I can remember all that ... just in case someone asks—you know, the neighbours or someone.

Eric Helen.

Helen No, let me try, Eric—you know how I like to try. (*She closes her eyes, concentrating*) You were driving home late after a business meeting with a Mr Bournemouth of Potters Bar Limited when a fly, which had entered the car despite your having taking the precaution of closing all the windows, flew into your eye. In an effort to avert what could have been a serious road accident, you turned off into a side road which subsequently turned out to be a private lane leading to a farm, switched off your lights to preserve the battery, took off your glasses and were totally occupied in removing the fly from your eye when you were struck from behind by a large lorry—the impact being such that you had to be cut out of the wreckage by the local fire brigade who first advised you to remove your trousers. (*She opens her eyes, pleased with herself*) There. (*But she remembers*) Oh yes ... luckily you had a witness. A Mrs O'Connell who has only recently joined the company and needed experience in the field and so you took her out in your car and were giving it to her. (*She beams*) How's that?

Eric Very good, Helen. Now, if you don't mind ... I'm quite exhausted.

Helen You'd like me to go.

Eric If you don't mind, Helen.

Helen No, of course I don't mind, Eric. You're going to need all the rest you can get. (*She stands, putting the plate of trifle on the cabinet and the rest of the things into her basket*) It'll be a long time before all that plaster and things come off. You'll be quite helpless. I shall have to attend to your every little whim. (*She leans over and lightly kisses his bandaged brow*)

During the following, she mops his mouth with the napkin which is still round his neck, thereby stopping any attempt he is making to protest at what she is saying

I tell you what I'm going to do: as I'm early, I'm going to pop upstairs to the Edith Cavell Ward and see if Mrs O'Connell has come out of her coma. She'll probably be a bit confused—it'll be nice for her to have me put her in the picture. And her husband, if he's there. You know—visiting.

Eric (*finally managing*) Helen . . .

But she is already kissing his brow again

Helen I've left you some trifle, you love my trifle, I know you do. Perhaps someone can give it to you later on. 'Bye then, Eric. (*She makes to leave but stops*) On second thoughts, you can have it now. (*She takes up the plate of trifle and pushes it into his face where it remains*) I'll bring you another one tomorrow. 'Bye.

She exits L, briskly

Eric remains motionless as the hospital noises fade up

A Nurse enters DR, pulls the curtains around the bed, and exits R

Keeping Mum

The Lights change so that the bed R containing the sleeping Old Woman is illuminated. The hospital noises fade and the handbell rings

After a moment, Pauline enters, UR. She is drawn, neat, fastidious. It is raining outside and she wears a raincoat. She pauses in the doorway to shake out an umbrella

She moves in and stands for a moment, looking at the motionless Old Woman as though uncertain. She props the umbrella up against the bedside cabinet and puts down her large bag. She moves closer to the Old Woman, cranking herself up for the ordeal

Pauline (*bending low; quietly but cheerfully*) Hallo dear, how are you feeling? Feeling a bit better are you? You certainly look a bit brighter, there's some colour in your cheeks. And they've done your hair, haven't they, it looks so much nicer, really pretty. (*She is gently touching the old woman's hair*) Who did it for you, the little Irish one?

The Old Woman raises an arm, murmuring soundlessly. Pauline takes the hand in both of hers and leans close, gently stroking the Old Woman's hand during the following

What's that, dear? No, it's Friday, today's Friday. Mmm? No, you mustn't worry about that, every day's the same when you're stuck in a silly old bed, aren't they? Yes. That's right, you close your eyes and I'll just sit here for a few minutes and keep you company, mm?

She continues to stroke the Old Woman's hand for a moment, then lowers it gently and moves to sit in the chair

Sorry I'm a bit late, the buses were all over the place. I left at twenty-five past, would you believe. They're always unreliable on a Friday so I thought: right, I'll allow myself another twenty minutes, that should be ample. Nothing like it. I said to him, quite politely, why are you so late, what's the excuse this time? The look on his face, you'd have thought I'd asked him the secret of the universe. In Swahili. We've got two drivers off sick, he said. I didn't pursue it. The truth is, of course, it's raining and we all know what that means, don't we? Two or three drops and they're loath to leave the depot, public transport my eye.

Slight pause

God knows when I'll get the car back. I phoned the insurance people this morning. It's in the pipeline, they said. It's been in the pipeline for over a month, I said, why don't you consult Dyno-Rod? That's what I should have said, anyway. They're quick enough about asking for the premium but when it comes to paying out . . . I was quite lost without that car for the first week or two. I'd forgotten what buses were all about. And the fares. I don't know how people do it, I really don't. Dennis is absolutely right. We take far too much for granted. You don't know how lucky you are, he says. I do now. Anyway. Here I am.

It has all come quickly but now the flow dries up. This moment. She looks around at the cabinet. During the following, she gets up to tidy the top of the cabinet, putting tissues, the used paper cup and straw, etc., into the wastebag which hangs inside the cabinet door. All for something to do

Look at this, they haven't cleared your cup away. Oh dear, you haven't touched it again. You must drink, you know, plenty of fluids they said, you must drink plenty of fluids. (*Confidentially*) You know what I think it is—I think it's those straws they give you. You don't like those straws, do you, that's what it is, you're not a baby, are you, you can manage, of course you can. Let's see what we can do when the trolley comes round, shall we? Nasty old straws, who wants to drink out of a nasty old straw, eh? Course you don't. Anyway. Let's have a bit of a tidy up, shall we, get rid of some of this nasty old rubbish. You'll be needing some more tissues by the look of it, I'll have a word with Nurse. Oh dear, look at this, someone's left the top off your water—when did they last change it, can you remember?

She covers the top of the jug with a tissue

There now, that's better, isn't it, we can see where we are now, can't we?

She sits, not facing the bed, more out front. She flicks imaginary pieces of fluff from her clothing: small, birdlike movements. A moment

It's nice and quiet this afternoon. Last week it was like Paddington Station. I expect they get their busy periods like everyone else. I don't suppose the nurses are complaining. Dennis says they like to have a clear out at weekends so that all these doctors can go off yachting or whatever it is they do. Still. Good luck to them, they work hard enough.

A moment

Were you in this cubicle when you first came in, I can't remember, isn't that awful? I had it on my mind all last night, God knows why but I was trying to picture which cubicle you were in at the beginning and do you know I couldn't for the life of me remember. I know the bed was round

the other way and they moved it because of the radiator but . . . All last
night, couldn't get it out of my mind. In the end I had to put the radio on
really loud and do a great pile of ironing. Mind you, it needed it, it's been
piling up for weeks. I just haven't felt like doing it, there didn't seem
any . . .

Who's on today, I wonder. There was no-one in the office. The telephone
was ringing away and no-one was taking a blind bit of notice. I nearly
answered it myself. Well it's not very nice, is it, phoning up to find out
how someone is and not even getting a reply. It doesn't exactly fill you
with confidence. People worry, it's only natural. Look at that time I
phoned intensive care. After the operation. You go home and get some
rest, Mrs Marley, they said—if anything happens we'll let you know, if
not you can phone first thing in the morning. What happens? I telephone
and I can't even get a reply from the switchboard. I was nearly out of my
mind. I've got to go to that hospital, I said, anything might have
happened. For God's sake, Pauline, he said, if anything's happened they
would have phoned. I don't care about that, I said, I want to go now—
now!

Her hands have tightened into fists as she has been re-living her anxiety. A
moment

Poor Dennis. It's been so hard for him. He's had the both of us to worry
about. I can say it now, and I mean it, but there have been times when I've
been terrible to him, said some terrible things. You see, when someone's
been ill as long as you have . . . I mean, it's not your fault, no-one's saying
it's your fault, but . . . I just took it out on him, I suppose. Oh well. It's all
settled now, it's all . . . sorted itself out.

A moment. She realizes she has been twisting the wedding ring on her finger

I popped in downstairs on the way in. Into intensive care. I like to say
hallo, they were so nice. They still have a good laugh about that night,
you know. Talk about strong as an ox, Mrs Marley—we've never seen
anything like it, will-power isn't in it. I said, she's always been strong-
willed, my mother. I suppose she had to be really, with someone like
Daddy for a husband, all that money trouble and gambling and everything. Strange how he took to gambling. He'd gamble on anything. It's a
disease like anything else, I suppose.

A moment. From somewhere, the distant sound of a telephone ringing

Tea trolley should be here soon. I wonder if I can persuade her to give me
a cup, I'm parched, I really am. I could have some of yours, I suppose, but
it's not really fair to mess up their charts. Sister said to me, we really have
to be very accurate about the amount of fluid she's taking otherwise it's a
complete waste of time.

She was quite short with me actually. Mind you, she looked tired, very
tired. And I think she's having problems with her son. I heard her talking
to the little Polish one. I'm beginning to sound like a right little busybody,
aren't I? Oh dear. You can't help hearing things when you've been sitting

around in corridors like I have for the past—what is it—eleven weeks. Eleven weeks, my God. Three months ago I didn't know this place existed and now I could find my way here with my eyes closed. And sometimes I do, sometimes I feel I'm on automatic. Dennis says, for God's sake give it a rest, she'll understand, I mean, good God, it's not as if she even knows you're there half the time . . . I said to him, I'm all she's got, she expects it . . . and you would, wouldn't you, you've always expected me to . . .

That's how I crashed the car, I suppose. I was so tired, doing everything by numbers. They said, we think she's going, Mrs Marley, we think perhaps you should come in. Thank God it was two o'clock in the morning and only me involved. I should have let him drive me in. He just lost patience, I suppose. I can't blame him. And not a scratch on me. I wish I could say the same for the rotten car.

First thing you said when you came out of the anaesthetic: where is she, you said. They couldn't believe it, half an hour after a major operation and you were demanding attention . . . She should be out for hours, they said, but there you were, eyes open, fighting to stay awake, forty-eight hours without sleep, they couldn't believe it, will of iron.

And what you called that poor doctor is nobody's business. I'm so sorry, Doctor, I said . . . Never you mind, Mrs Marley, he said, it's the anaesthetic, she's hallucinating and you should hear what some of them call me. There he is, trying to save your life and all he gets for his trouble is: get away from me, you ugly black bastard. A mouthful of tubes and still you can spit it out like you've always managed to spit it out. I demand to see the manager, you said, and he'd better not be a blackie like the rest of them. You thought you were in some foreign hotel. Bermuda, I think you said. Only why you should think of Bermuda, I've no idea. You've never been there and, as far as I know, never expressed the desire. Until then, of course. I suppose it must have been all those potted plants and dark faces.

They were so kind to you. We don't take any notice, they said. Besides, she's such a lovely old lady. I felt ashamed.

A moment. Then she looks towards the bed and reaches out to touch the hand resting on the cover

Your hands look nice. They look really nice since you've been in here. Someone's been doing your nails by the look of it. Like a young girl's. So soft and white.

She gently lets go of the hand and looks down at her own hands, turning away from the bed

That's what David said . . . I never realized what nice hands Gran has got, they're really nice, a really nice shape. He would have come to see you more often but it upset him so much, he's always hated hospitals. I remember that time I went in for my scrape. I had to say to him: for goodness sake, David. Go home you're making me a nervous wreck.

Thanks, Mum, he said, hope you feel better, and he was out of that room quicker than if I'd asked him to do the washing up.

I really enjoyed those four days in hospital. (*Smiling at the thought*) All that lovely rest. I should have been in for at least the week but that was the time you had your heart attack. Suspected heart attack, they were never really sure, were they? Anyway, there I was, on the run again.

You've always been very ... unfortunate in your timing, haven't you? Even on my wedding day you managed to get that terrible migraine and I remember when I was in the school play ...

She gets up suddenly, angrily, and moves forward two or three paces and looks up and down the corridor, giving herself time to calm

Trolley's late. You can hear it coming a mile away. It's got a life of its own, that trolley. Uncontrollable. I watched her the other day, careering down the corridor, ricochetting from one bed across to the other as though she was expecting them to light up, as though it was her personal pinball machine. Perhaps it is, perhaps it's her way of getting back.

She sits. A moment

I just wish more than anything I could get a good night's sleep. I take those pills the doctor gave me, but, I don't know, I drop off and half an hour later I'm wide-awake again. My brain just won't ... shut down. I could take more, I suppose, but I don't want to become dependent on them, I've seen what they can do.

Do you know, never a night goes by without I see Daddy. I mean I go to bed and I close my eyes and I see his face. It's been the same ever since he died, not like when he was ill, not like what he'd become, but as I remember him when I was about, oh, fifteen I suppose.

I can't remember you as you were. I try, I try to force a picture into my mind but all I ever see is you as you are now. I know what you were like, I remember so clearly, I mean I can talk about it, make a picture out of words ... but inside my head ...

You should have died. They should have let you die, I mean, what was the point? It's spread everywhere, they said, there's nothing we can do except ease the pain, two months, perhaps more, it's difficult to say at her age, sometimes they hang on. Does she know what it is, I said ... No? Then for God's sake don't tell her, she's terrified of death, she always has been, that's why she can't stand being on her own. If she asks, we'll tell her, they said ... if she doesn't ask, it's up to you. But you didn't ask. And I didn't tell you. Just day after day of coming here and pretending everything was going to be all right and going home and what could they give *me* for *my* pain?

I saw that fat woman on the way in. The one with the corset, the one that caused all that fuss. She's back in for a check-up, they'll be pleased. D'you remember how she refused to take her clothes off? I am not taking my clothes off and that is final, she said. She did make me laugh, that sister: if you've got something I've never seen, Mrs Whatever-Your-Name-Is, I'll shoot it. We did laugh. If you've got something I've never seen, I'll shoot it.

She laughs and takes a handkerchief from her bag. A moment

He's gone. Dennis. He's left me. Four days ago. Don't go to that hospital, he said, I want to talk to you. What about, I said—I already had my coat on. Just sit down, he said, I need to talk to you. Don't be silly, I said, you know I've got to go, you know she expects it. He didn't argue. He just said . . . Yes, that's right, you go to the hospital. When I got back there was a suitcase in the hall and he was sitting in the kitchen with his coat on— What's this, I said, what's happening? He said, I can't stand it any more, that's what's happening, Pauline . . . I've done my best, for months I've done my best . . . but I can't stand it any more, you need help and I can't give it to you.

A moment

When I say he's left me, I'm not saying it's permanent, I'm saying . . .

A moment

You couldn't stay on your own, there was no way you could look after yourself—we agreed. I talked about putting you into one of those homes but he knew I didn't really mean it. You'd never forgive yourself, you can't put her into one of those places, he said, have you seen them? I did have a look at one or two. I just wanted to cry. She's your mother, he said, we'll look after her. If it gets too bad, all right, then we'll have to think of something else.

Four months you were with us. Four months with the smell of death in every room. It was the ups and downs that made it so hard . . . One minute sitting up all night, waiting for you to die, the next minute running up and down those stairs, you ringing that bell he fixed up . . . where's my drink, where's that sandwich you promised me, you're no daughter of mine, you don't care about me . . . I could cope with it when I thought you were going but to see you sitting up in that bed demanding this demanding that, looking at me like I was a skivvy . . . God how I wanted you to die.

It was me who sent for the ambulance that night, me who couldn't cope any more. He said, we've had her this long, you'll never forgive yourself if she dies in that hospital, but you didn't know where you were any more . . . you were in a coma, all those drugs they kept giving you, all those injections . . . I just couldn't face what I had to do any more . . . I couldn't face seeing those sores all over your poor body . . . I couldn't face changing one more sheet . . . I'm phoning for the ambulance, I said, it's the right thing I know it is. They were there in ten minutes. Only young boys really. They were so gentle with you.

You looked so . . . tiny. Like an empty . . .

They didn't think you'd last the night. But even then you wouldn't give in, hour after hour I sat there, day after day, night after night, just looking at you. I went home that night—you were very low, they let me stay 'til, oh, it must have been two in the morning. I'd been in the house ten minutes and the phone rang. We're very sorry, Mrs Marley. I must have said my goodbyes to you a hundred times but when I should have been here ... half an hour I'd been gone. We're very sorry, they said. I came straight back to see you—he tried to stop me but ... I had to see you. You'd struggled so hard and then ... just slipped away. She didn't wake up, they said, it was very peaceful, the best way really. Are you sure, I said. Are you sure she didn't ...

She breaks down and recovers and wipes her eyes with the handkerchief

I didn't cry at the funeral. It didn't seem to have anything to do with me ... or you ... or anything, really.

A moment

Next day, I brought a big tin of coffee into the nurses—they'd been so very kind and it was the least I could do to say thank you. They were very pleased. Then, on the Friday I think it was, I was out shopping and I saw the bus pulling up at the stop and ... Anyway. I can't expect him to understand, it's what you have to do, isn't it? But you understand, don't you, you know why I'm here ... you've always ... I wanted to say I love you, you know that, don't you? Mum ... I wanted to say it.

She cries. The Old Woman stirs in the bed, raising a feeble arm. Pauline recovers quickly and gets up and moves to lean over the Old Woman, taking the hand in her two hands

Hallo, dear, how are you feeling? It's me, Mrs Marley, I was just passing and I know you don't get many visitors so I thought I'd just pop in and see how you were. Mmmm? Mrs Marley. My mother was in the next bed—you used to have those little chats. Mmmm? That's right, yes, I came yesterday. Close your eyes and I'll just sit here for a few minutes and keep you company 'til the trolley comes round, eh?

She gently lowers the hand and sits, looking out front again. During the following, the Lights slowly fade to Black-out

I would have been here earlier but the buses were all over the place. I left at twenty-five past, would you believe. They've always been unreliable on a Friday so I thought, right, I'll allow myself another twenty minutes, that should be ample ...

The hospital noises build

Pauline and the Old Woman exit in the darkness and Fiona and Naomi, Julia and Maureen enter

Showbusiness

The hospital noises fade. Silence for a moment and then Fiona's voice

Fiona Bums. Bums bums bums! All right all right we'll go again—my fault—sorry about the language and here we go and Operating Theatre, St Leonard's Hospital, May fifteenth.

Fiona's head and shoulders are illuminated in a square of light—as though it's a television screen. She is black, very attractive, very well-dressed, and is holding a stick mike

(*Immediately*) Ten years ago, in this very theatre, Naomi Strelitz was a junior doctor assisting at her first operation. Today, she is one of our country's leading transplant surgeons.

Her spotlight goes out as, at the same time, a second, similar spotlight illuminates Naomi's head and shoulders. She is wearing operating gown and hat, has her gloved hands raised palms towards her. She is well-versed in media technique

Naomi Hallo.

The spotlight goes out

(*Immediately*) All right?
Fiona Super.

An area lights up and we see Naomi, Fiona, Julia and Maureen. Maureen has a small ENG camera on her shoulder. Julia has a sound boom and various other bits and pieces of sound and lighting equipment. Fiona is checking her face in a large mirror. Naomi is carefully taking off the hat and gloves

Naomi Can someone help me off with this gown?
Fiona Be a love, Jules.

Julia somewhat gracelessly helps Naomi out of the gown

Maureen Where to now?
Fiona (*referring to her clipboard*) Umm ... straight to the ward I think. (*To Julia*) It is all cleared with Sister, is it, Jules?

Julia gives her a hard look

Yes, of course—sorry.

By now Naomi is out of the gown: she is very attractive and well-groomed. She takes the mirror from Fiona and checks her hair in it during the following

Naomi How much longer will you be needing me this morning?
Fiona Oh—half an hour should cover it wouldn't you say, Maureen?
Maureen Depends how fast the lighting and sound department can get her arse into gear.

Julia looks up hatefully from her lamps

Julia Slag.
Maureen Slut.
Naomi (*giving the mirror to Julia*) I'll have to follow you on—I've got a few calls to make.

Fiona No problem—(*her professional smile*)—the patients must come first.
Naomi What? Oh—no—telephone calls—my stupid secretary has double-booked a lunch appointment.

Naomi exits briskly

Maureen Tough titty.

Julia holds up the gown and mask

Julia Are these theirs or wardrobe?

The area goes to a Black-out. The Lights come up on the UL *bed*

> *A Male Nurse enters and pulls back the curtains to reveal the* UL *bed which contains Mr Darbon. The Nurse exits*

Mr Darbon lies, slightly propped up in the bed. He is an elderly man who has dozed off listening to the hospital radio programme on his headphones, while at the same time taking oxygen through nasal prongs

Fiona enters the ward, being filmed by Maureen and sound-recorded on the boom by Julia

Fiona This . . . is the Peter Smethurst Wing. So-called after the first surgeon to perform a heart transplant here at Saint Leonard's Hospital. Each of the patients in this wing is either recovering from, or about to undergo, intensive surgery. Each of them has either looked, or is looking, into the face of death. Nothing unusual about that, you might say. But for one of them, there is a place in medical history. OK that's that one—happy Maureen, happy everyone?—let's move on then, shall we? (*She moves to the bedside. Bending down to him*) Mr—(*she checks the clipboard*)—Darbon?

No response. She sighs, looks around for help, almost prods him, but instead raises one of the earpieces—delicately, as though fearing infection

Fiona Boyce, Mr Darbon—WTV.

His eyes open and he smiles at her. During the following, Maureen moves around the bed, looking for the best camera angles, while Julia sets up her bits and pieces: a spotlight etc.

Darbon Is that the time then, is it?
Fiona Good-morning.
Darbon Only you never know nowadays, do you?
Fiona Sorry?
Darbon It was just the same last time I was in.
Fiona Fiona *Boyce*, Mr Darbon—WTV.
Darbon (*face lighting up*) I know you.
Fiona Good.
Darbon I thought you was Basket Making but you're not, are you?
Fiona (*beaming*) Sorry—no.
Darbon No, course you're not—you're the one from Ear, Nose and Froat. Open wide. (*He opens his mouth wide*)

Fiona Hasn't anyone—spoken to you?

Darbon All done? (*He clamps his mouth shut and adjusts his headphones*)
You're very kind. You're all very kind, you people. (*He points to the
headphones*) Tell you who you don't hear a lot of lately: Elsie and Doris
Waters.

Fiona (*long-suffering*) I'm from the television, Mr Darbon. We're doing a
programme about you. About your operation. Someone should have
spoken to you.

The Male Nurse enters L

Nurse—someone was supposed to speak to him.

Nurse They did. I did—we all did. It's whether he was listening.

Seeing the Nurse, Darbon gives a big thumbs-up and a smile

You drift, don't you, Walter?

Darbon I tell you another one—Ronnie Ronalde.

Nurse You're right there, Walter. (*To Fiona*) One minute he's right on the
ball, next minute he's miles away. Years away.

Fiona Look— sorry—but I've got a crew waiting out there and we're on an
incredibly tight schedule—I need his permission.

Nurse (*raising one of the earpieces*) They want you to go on television,
Walter—they want to make you famous.

Darbon Yes I know, the lady spoke to me about it yesterday. Very nice. (*He
goes back to his radio listening*)

Nurse (*to Fiona*) See what I mean?

Fiona Thank you. So we can, er . . . (*She mimes "come in"*)

Nurse (*spreading his hands*) Whatever you want—that's what they said.

Fiona (*calling and indicating*) OK crew, here we go!

Nurse You won't be needing me, will you?

Fiona (*her big smile*) I'll give you a shout if we do, OK? (*The smile changes
to a look of meaningful intimacy; squeezing his forearm*) Thanks for all
your help. (*Immediately turning to Maureen*) What I thought was: start
with a wide angle from here . . . (*And she continues describing to Maureen
how she sees the camera shots*)

Nurse (*leaning close to Darbon*) I'll come back later for your autograph, all
right, Walter?

Darbon gives him his smile and thumbs-up

The Nurse exits R

Fiona You don't like it.

Maureen If I came from here, I could get what's-his-name and the equipment and some of the window.

Fiona Outside which life goes on as per . . . much better—*much* better.

Maureen I'll need some light to balance up.

Fiona OK, Jules?

*Julia gives her the hard look and sets up the spotlight tripod as Fiona smiles
down at Darbon and continues*

All we'll be doing this morning, Mr—er—Darbon—is a couple of small inserts—the main stuff will be done in the operating theatre when you'll be ... so you won't ... OK? (*But she is already assuming the proposed camera angle*) What would be nice would be if we could find someone to lounge around out there—don't you think, Maureen? Between this window and the blue Fiesta with the roof-rack—say a young couple—having a kiss or a sandwich or something. (*And, to Darbon*) Oh, and in case you're wondering—we won't be shooting in sequence and the cutaway shots will be picked up later back at base—OK?

Darbon gives the thumbs-up

(*To Maureen*) It's a pity he doesn't look more—ill.
Maureen Have a word with the make-up department—she makes everything look like a corpse.
Julia Oh yes, very funny, ha ha.
Fiona If only he looked more—blue or something.
Maureen We might be able to tweak some in later.
Fiona (*squeezing her forearm*) Be super if you could.

The Nurse enters

Nurse Everything OK?
Fiona Super.

He is about to go

Oh Nurse ... (*She links arms with him and guides him away to speak intimately*) What surprises me is how ... well, how well he looks.
Nurse Oh yeah?
Fiona I have to think in terms of visual impact, you see.
Nurse Oh yeah?
Fiona How he looks before the operation ... and how he looks after it.
Nurse If there is an after it.
Fiona I was wondering about that thing sticking out of his nose.
Nurse That's his oxygen, his lungs are dodgy.
Fiona Could he not be wearing one of those—(*she mimes*)—mask things?
Nurse You want him to wear a mask.
Fiona They look so much more ... I mean unless it ... ?
Nurse If that's what you want. (*He goes to Darbon*) They want you to wear a mask, Walter—it makes you look prettier.

Darbon gives him the thumbs-up and the Nurse exchanges a clear plastic mask for the nasal prongs during the following

Fiona There's nothing else you can attach to him, is there? Tubes or something?
Nurse They're already attached.
Fiona Well if they could be—arranged—so that they're in shot.
Nurse They want to see your tubes, Walter.

Darbon says something behind the mask

Fiona Sorry?
Nurse He said his brother was on the buses.
Fiona Oh—right.

She gives a thumbs-up to Darbon who gives one back. During the following, the Nurse adjusts the bed clothing so that the various tubes leading from the instruments are more visible

Naomi enters. She looks somewhat pre-occupied

Naomi Look, something's cropped up—(*she switches on the bedside smile for Darbon*)—good-morning, Mr Darbon, lovely to see you—(*and switches it straight off again*)—so if we can make this as brief as possible— thank you.
Fiona No problem.
Naomi OK, where would you like me?
Fiona Bedside—in the chair—chair please, Jules . . .

In fetching the chair, Julia has to squeeze past Maureen

Julia (*icily*) Excuse me.
Maureen Oh yes—I was forgetting the size of the hips.
Julia Slag.
Maureen Slut.
Nurse (*to Fiona, of Julia and Maureen*) What's with those two?
Fiona Lovers' tiff.
Nurse Oh. Oh.

Julia arranges the chair and Naomi sits

Naomi Left profile, please. (*She shows her left profile*)
Fiona OK, Jules? And a little closer d'you think, Maureen? Yes, a tidge closer please, Jules. That's fine.
Naomi How's the make-up?
Maureen Make-up.
Fiona Make-up please, Jules.

Julia gives Naomi a quick powdering

I'll just knock off a quick wildtrack. (*She takes up her stick mike*) Wildtrack number—(*she checks against clipboard*)—fourteen and here we go and . . .

A spotlight on Darbon as she continues directly

Walter Darbon will be the first patient in this country to undergo a quadruple transplant operation. Heart, lungs, liver, and kidney—and cut!

The spotlight goes out

Naomi So it's just a simple two-shot of me breaking the news to him, is it?
Maureen That's what it says on the schedule.
Fiona (*to Naomi*) All we've time for, I'm afraid.
Naomi Cries out for a couple of BCU's.

Fiona We'll probably cheat some in later.
Naomi And he's going to be lying back like that, is he?
Fiona What have you in mind?
Naomi Because if he is, all we're going to see of me is the back of my head.

She turns her head to look directly at Darbon and prove her point. Darbon gives her his thumbs-up

Fiona Good point.
Naomi Unless that's what all you want to see—the back of my head.

She shows it again. And again Darbon gives her the thumbs-up. Julia has set her lights up and plugged them into the power pack. She turns them on. Darbon stares into them

Julia Ask her how that is.

Fiona looks to Maureen

Maureen It'll do.
Nurse Not in the patient's eyes, please.

Julia turns the spotlight on to Naomi

Naomi (*irritably*) Well?
Maureen Can't we sit him forward?
Fiona Jules . . .
Nurse Uh-uh—I'll do it. (*To Naomi*) You want him forward more.
Naomi Just for half a minute—thank you, Nurse.
Nurse You're going for a ride, Walter. (*He starts cranking up the bed*)

Darbon gives the thumbs up

Fiona All right, Maureen?
Nurse Say when.
Naomi (*leaning into Darbon*) Small suggestion, Mr Darbon—when you look at me—not in the eyes—at the right ear—OK?

He gives her the thumbs-up and says something behind the mask

What was that?
Nurse He says his brother-in-law worked for Kodak. Just after the war.
Naomi (*to Darbon*) Well you'll know all about these things then, won't you? I can see I shall have to watch my step. (*She "smiles" but angles the chair a little more forward*)
Maureen (*looking through the camera*) When.

The Nurse stops cranking. Darbon is in an almost-upright position

Nurse OK?
Fiona OK, Maureen?
Maureen Lights.
Fiona Lights please, Jules.

Julia turns the lights

(*To the Nurse, indicating for him to get out of the shot*) If you could umm
... (*She grips his forearm briefly*) Thank you. (*To Naomi*) If we could have
a little sound check ... ?

Naomi Eenie meenie minee mo, catch a ... testing, testing, one two three,
testing.

Fiona OK, Jules?

*Julia is crouching "out of shot" with the microphone, and looking at the
control box*

Julia OK for sound.

Maureen What about *him*?

Naomi There won't be any need for him to say anything, will there? All he
has to do is react, surely?

Fiona (*leaning into Darbon*) We're going to take a picture of Mrs Strelitz
telling you about your operation. All you need do is look like you
understand. That's quite clear, isn't it?

Darbon says something behind the mask

Sorry?

Nurse He said heart, lungs, liver and bacon.

Darbon gives the thumbs-up

Fiona OK, everyone? Record.

Maureen Running ... (*But*) What about the headphones?

Fiona Strike the headphones.

Julia sighs and takes off Darbon's headphones and gets back into position

OK, Maureen; OK, everyone? (*She leans close to the microphone*) Interior
Ward May Fifteenth—(*and ducks out of shot*)—and—action!

Naomi and Darbon are highlighted and Naomi swings smoothly into action

Naomi Well, Mr Darbon—Walter—it's been a long wait for both of us ...
but at last I can give you the good news: we have a donor for you and it's
all systems go tomorrow morning.

*She takes one of Darbon's hands and squeezes it emotionally. Darbon says
something behind the mask*

Fiona And cut!

The camera lights go out

Super.

Naomi All right?

Fiona Super.

Naomi What was that he said?

Nurse He said "very nice".

Maureen We can get rid of it in the edit.

Fiona OK, let's set up for the alternative—OK, Jules?

Naomi Mirror please.

Julia passes her the mirror and checks her equipment during the following

Nurse (*quietly, to Fiona*) I didn't know they were operating on him tomorrow.
Fiona No, no, they're not—we're getting it in now to save time later.
Julia OK!
Maureen Hoo-ray.
Fiona Record.
Maureen Running.

Fiona leans into the microphone which Julia is holding and Naomi and Darbon are highlighted again

Fiona Interior Ward May Fifteenth Alternative—(*ducking out of shot*)—and action!
Naomi (*swinging into action again*) Bad news again I'm afraid, Walter. We've lost our donor—yes I know old chap—but I won't give up, I promise you ... I won't give up.

She takes Darbon's hand in exactly the same way as before and he mumbles something behind the mask

Fiona And cut!

The highlights go out

    Super.
Naomi All right?
Fiona Super.
Naomi What was that he said?
Nurse He said, "very nice".
Maureen We can get rid of it in the edit. (*She puts down the camera*)
Fiona (*looking at the clipboard*) OK what's next?
Maureen (*pointing to her watch*) Coffee.
Fiona Ah—yes—right.

Maureen is already making towards the exit

    (*Calling somewhat impotently after her*) If you could umm ...

Julia is on her way out

    Um ... five minutes—OK, Jules?

    Maureen and Julia exit separately

Nurse All right if he has his music back?
Fiona What? Oh—yes—fine.

The Nurse puts the headphones back on Darbon

    Sorry about this. (*She tries a smile*) Union Rules, OK? (*Immediately serious again*) What we *can* do—what I'd *like* to do ...
Naomi (*to the Nurse, suddenly*) All right if I use the phone?
Nurse Certainly.

Naomi exits, leaving Fiona feeling a bit of a chump

Fiona She's terribly busy of course. Well, you all are. All you people. I really do think you deserve every penny you get—well, you probably saw that feature I did on it.

Nurse (*lowering the angle of the bed*) You know what *she's* worried about, don't you? Fisher.

Fiona Fisher?

Nurse Fisher. Over at the Gladstone.

Fiona Fisher. Oh—*Fisher*—the one who did the heart and lung transplant on that ten month old Armenian child . . .

Nurse Six month old Turkish child.

Fiona What about him? Sorry.

Nurse (*jerking his head towards the door*) She's got word that he's lining up a quadruple.

A spotlight illuminates Naomi's head and shoulders, using the telephone

Naomi (*shouting*) He's what? He's bloody *what?*

The spotlight goes out on Naomi

Fiona (*sensing a story*) How d'you mean: got word?

Nurse They've both done the triple, right? Heart, lungs and liver. And they're both desperate to be first with the quadruple.

A spotlight, as though a TV screen, illuminates a Woman holding a newspaper

Woman (*reading*) "A Woman's Place Is In The Operating Theatre—Top Surgeon Speaks."

A second similar spotlight illuminates another Woman holding a newspaper

2nd Woman (*reading*) "Transplant Surgeon In Midnight Mercy Dash."

The spotlights go out on the two Women

Nurse (*continuing straight on*) Now then—she's got her recipient—Walter here—*and* a potential donor . . . he's got his recipient but he's still looking for his donor—but now it's coming through the grapevine that he might have found one.

Fiona So what we have . . . is a race to see who can stick the scalpel in first.

Nurse (*to Darbon*) You're her South Pole, aren't you, Walter?

Darbon gives him the thumbs-up and says something behind the mask

Fiona What did he say?

Nurse He said, "very nice".

Naomi enters, pre-occupied

Fiona and the Nurse exchange a look

Naomi Sorry.

Fiona Problems?

Naomi Problems? No—just . . . where were we?
Nurse I'll be in my office. (*He makes to go*)
Naomi Nurse . . . there might be a call for me—let me know as soon as it
  comes through, will you?
Nurse *Certainly*, Mrs Strelitz.

  The Nurse exits

*Fiona and Naomi sit either side of the bed, ignoring Darbon who will look from
one to the other as they speak*

Fiona What I'd like to do is get in a few wildtracks, OK? Voice overs that
  we can use as and when——
Naomi Yes, yes, I have done this sort of thing before, you know.
Fiona (*an edge*) Yes, of course, you have —sorry.
Naomi Just let's . . . (*She indicates "get on with it"*)

*By now Fiona has her stick mike which she will shove back and forth across
Darbon as she refers to her clipboard*

Fiona If you could sum up the present situation *vis-à-vis* the donor—OK?
  And . . . (*She indicates for Naomi to begin, holding the mike out to her*)
Naomi (*immediately leaning in across Darbon*) The donor—the victim of a
  motor-cycle accident—has been on a life-support machine for the past
  three weeks . . .
Fiona Don't think we should be specific about the date—sorry—and I think
  we said "unfortunate victim", OK? and . . . (*She indicates "go"*)
Naomi The donor—the unfortunate victim of a motor-cycle accident—is at
  present on a life support machine and, sadly, with no hope, barring
  miracle, of physical recovery. Tests for brain death are carried out at
  regular intervals. (*To Fiona, directly*) I understand you've already spoken
  to the next-of-kin.
Fiona Yesterday.

*Spotlights, in the form of TV screens illuminate the next of kin: Mother and
Father. She wears hat and spectacles, he wears a trilby hat*

Father We spent a long time thinking about this, but we are now agreed:
  when our son is pronounced brain-dead, his organs may be used as
  necessary.
Mother It's what he would have wanted.
Father If our son's death means that others may benefit, then his mother
  and I——
Fiona (*voice over*) Cut!

The spotlights go out on the Mother and Father

And you've no idea when that will be?
Naomi God only knows what's keeping him going. But no: there's nothing I
  can do until they officially pull the plug on him—then it's all stations go—
  and that can't come soon enough, I can tell you.
Fiona (*of Darbon*) For him you mean?

Naomi What? Oh—him—yes—of course. This bit is all off the record, I take it?

Fiona Oh yes, absolutely.

Darbon says something behind his mask. They both look at him

How ill *is* he?

Naomi Well you've only got to look at his record—or better still, speak to his daughter and her husband.

Spotlights illuminate the Son-in-law and Daughter. The Son-in-law wears a moustache and spectacles, the Daughter wears a headscarf

Daughter He's been steadily going downhill ever since Mum died.

Son-in-law They're all right as long as they're together . . .

Daughter But as soon as one goes . . .

Son-in-law Like your clutch, really—as soon as your clutch goes, pound to a penny you can say goodbye to your gearbox.

Daughter Since he come to live with us he's been in hospital five times.

Son-in-law First his pacemaker.

Daughter Then that bag thing.

Son-in-law Then they gave him a new hip.

Daughter Then a new leg.

Son-in-law He's got more plastic in him than a box of Lego.

Daughter Last time they operated on him, they wanted him to sign this form donating his body to medical science.

Son-in-law He refused on the grounds that most of it wasn't his body anyway.

The spotlights go out on the Son-in-law and Daughter. The Nurse enters

Nurse Mrs Strelitz—(*miming*) phone.

Naomi Right. *Right.*

Naomi exits quickly

The Nurse is about to go

Fiona Nurse . . . you will er, you will keep me informed, won't you?

Nurse (*jerking his head towards the door*) You mean . . .

Fiona It *is* in the public interest.

Nurse (*an edge*) Oh—yes—right—*right.*

She squeezes his forearm and gives him the meaningful look

Fiona Thank you.

The Nurse exits

Fiona looks towards the other door, then at her watch, then sees Darbon looking at her and raises one of his earpieces

Sorry about this—coffee break—shouldn't be much longer.

He gives her the thumbs-up and she lowers his earpiece and takes up the stick mike

What I'll do is knock off a few more wildtracks for the talking heads sequence. (*She refers to her clipboard and sits on the bed alongside Darbon*) OK here we go, intro, talking heads and—"Mrs Strelitz, what would you say to those people who argue that operations such as this are a complete waste of time?"

A spotlight illuminates Naomi

Naomi I'd say piss off. (*But*) Can we go again, please?

The spotlight goes out and another spotlight illuminates the Critic who wears horn-rimmed spectacles

Critic The surgical unit is given a budget which enables the team to do x number of operations—an operation like this will mop up the surgical budget for the entire year.

The spotlight goes out and another spotlight illuminates Naomi

Naomi Hospitals compete as service providers. If this operation is a success then it will attract more patients, which means more money.

The spotlight goes out as another spotlight illuminates the Daughter

Daughter I said to her: yes I see that, Doctor, but the thing is—what's the point of giving him a new heart if his liver is on the blink? So they give him a new liver and his bladder goes bust. Give my father a new heart and he could be wetting the bed for another ten years and I'm not sure that I could stand it.

Another spotlight illuminates the Critic

Critic All right, let's be perfectly frank: keeping this man alive is simply not cost-effective.

A spotlight illuminates Naomi

Naomi The fundamental object of the medical profession is the relief of suffering and the preservation of life.

A spotlight illuminates a Woman Critic

Woman Critic Medical advancement has made it possible to keep a dying person alive almost indefinitely. Death no longer occurs—it is managed!

Daughter Someone has to die though, don't they? Even if it's just so they can borrow a part or two to get someone else going.

Naomi The boundaries of medical science are being pushed back further and further and we—this man and I—are the trail blazers!

Darbon gives the thumbs-up sign

The spotlights go out on Naomi, the Critic, the Daughter and the Woman Critic

Maureen and Julia enter

Julia (*entering*) I never said that.

Maureen Well what did you say?
Julia All I said was, look what the Wicked Fairy has done to Bonnie Langford.
Maureen Meaning what?
Julia Meaning that beige is not your colour.
Maureen It was not beige, it was puce.
Julia Could've fooled *me*.
Maureen Slut.
Julia Slag.
Maureen Where are we? (*She's already setting up her camera*)
Fiona (*referring to the clipboard*) Shot ... twenty-seven—the personal statement.

Maureen directs the camera at Darbon

Maureen You want him like that, do you?
Fiona Umm, no, sitting up.
Maureen Props!
Julia The nurse is supposed to do it.
Fiona Yes, you're absolutely right, Jules, but the nurse is, err, doing something for me. So, umm, OK?

Julia scowls and cranks the bed the wrong way so that Darbon is completely flat. Julia realizes her mistake and cranks the other way, so that he is levered upright—too upright, in fact

(*Removing Darbon's headphones*) What I'd like you to do, Mr Darbon, is just say a few words—your personal message—just in case you don't surv——is there anything particular you'd like to say—under the circumstances?

Darbon nods and gives the thumbs-up

Fire away, then.
Julia I'm not ready, I'm not ready.
Maureen Always the drama queen.
Fiona Just a rehearsal, Jules, OK? OK, Mr Darbon? Keep a time check, will you, Jules—and—record.
Maureen Running.
Fiona Action. (*She points to him*)

Darbon starts to talk behind the mask

Maureen Sound!
Julia It's not me, it's the mask.
Maureen Typical—strike the mask!

Julia removes the oxygen mask

Fiona (*to Darbon*) Just for a jiffy—OK, everyone? And ... (*She points at Darbon*)
Darbon When I was a very young lad, I used to watch my father shaving. He used to stand there at the sink with just his trousers and singlet on.

Lathering up. Leathering his cut-throat. One morning I noticed these three hairs. These three hairs, sticking out the top of his shoulder. Three black hairs sticking out of his white skin. (*He touches his own shoulder*) I hated my father for those hairs. I hated him. Twenty years later and I'm shaving and suddenly I look in the mirror and there they are. Three—black—hairs. (*He lapses into silence*)

Fiona That's it, is it?

The Nurse enters, L, briskly

Nurse (*not unhappily*) It's happened.

Throughout the following, and unseen by the others, Darbon will become short of breath and grope to find the oxygen mask

Fiona (*going to the Nurse*) What?
Nurse Fisher's done a deal with the next-of-kin and the *News of the World*.

Fiona doesn't seem to understand

He's nicked her donor!

A tiny moment as it sinks in

Fiona OK, team—Plan B!

Fiona, Maureen and Julia swing into action, collecting up their gear

Naomi enters L, furious

Naomi Shit! (*She makes to exit DR*)
Fiona Go, Mo, Go!

Fiona is thrusting the stick mike under Naomi's nose and Maureen quickly gets into camera position and films

Mrs Strelitz—how do you feel now that you have lost out on the opportunity to perform the first——
Naomi (*still on the move*) I have no comment, no comment.
Fiona I'm sure our viewers would——
Naomi Piss off.

Naomi exits DR

Fiona immediately swings her mike, followed by Maureen and camera, on the Nurse

Fiona Nurse Littlejohn—you were one of the first to hear the news that——
Nurse You don't really think I'm going to discuss that *here*, do you? God you make me laugh, you people. (*He turns on his heel and makes for the door but stops*) Come through into my office—I can sit at my desk, miming an urgent phone call or the like.

The Nurse starts to exit, L, followed by Fiona and Maureen and Julia, who is now laden down with her equipment

(*As he goes*) What I suggest is you start on the wall chart and then pull back to big close-up me in heavy foreground . . . and you'd better do something about my eyelashes, they photograph something terrible.

They have all gone

Maureen (*off*) Make-up!
Julia (*off*) Lights!
Fiona (*off*) Action!

Silence after the whirl of activity, and then we become aware of the sound of Darbon's laboured breathing as he gropes for the mask, pulling it towards him by the tube as though pulling in a fish. He gets it to his mouth and sucks in air. A moment. Then he removes the mask

Darbon Oh well . . . that's show business. (*He puts the mask back on his mouth and closes his eyes*)

The sound of hospital noises comes up as the Lights fade slowly in on him, and then to a Black-out

CURTAIN

ACT II

Going Home

The same

Cheryl sits propped up in the UR *bed. She's in her mid-thirties and wears a knitted cardigan over her nightie. She is making half-hearted attempts to study the piece of paper she is holding, but her thoughts keep drifting away and she stares out into the distance. There is a sudden burst of laughter from unseen women and Cheryl turns her head towards them,* L, *smiling to herself. But then the smile fades as she becomes involved in her own thoughts again*

So that she is sitting, staring ahead, loosely holding the paper, as Tricia enters L. *She is black, wears a quality dressing-gown over her nightie. She is moving with extreme care, taking small steps, towards the* DR *bed*

Cheryl comes out of her thoughts and sees her. They smile at each other— easy, unforced, smiles

Cheryl You're moving well.
Tricia Watch out Zola Budd. (*She draws level with Cheryl's bed and stops*) How are you feeling today?
Cheryl Bit sore. You know.
Tricia All right for a chat?
Cheryl (*indicating her chair*) Please.
Tricia (*sitting carefully*) You certainly look a lot better than you did yesterday.
Cheryl Yes, I know—I felt terrible—I had a really high temperature—I felt really—you know—wrung out. All I wanted to do was sleep. They said it was an infection—the stitches.
Tricia Does that mean they'll be keeping you in longer?
Cheryl A couple of days, maybe. It really depends on how quickly it clears up.
Tricia Oh dear.
Cheryl (*quickly*) No, I don't mind. (*As though to explain*) I mean—you have to accept these things, don't you?

Hazel enters L. *She's in her dubious fifties, wears full make-up, tinted and immaculate hair, a bright dressing-gown, her handbag over one arm and her catheter bag in the other. She moves slowly and doesn't look at them directly or stop moving through the following*

Hazel It never rains but it pours, does it? I say it never rains but it pours.
Tricia What's happened?

Hazel Marion in number five. He's just phoned her—that husband of hers. She could tell from his voice that something was up. What is it, Marion? I said. Oh Hazel, she said, we've been burgled.

Both Tricia and Cheryl instinctively look L *towards the unseen Marion*

Tricia Oh, no.

Hazel Monday she loses her womb, Friday they take her furniture. *He's* gone to pieces, of course. Bang goes *her* rest when she gets home. I'm just popping down the shop to get her some barley sugars to cheer her up a bit—anything you want, is there, girls?

Tricia and Cheryl ad lib their "no thanks, Hazel"*'s*

Hazel exits DR

Then they both look again in the direction of the unseen Marion

Cheryl She gets so much bad luck, that woman.

Tricia Not very bright of him to tell her, I would have thought. Not *now*.

Cheryl You don't know though, do you? I mean, maybe if he hadn't told her ... (*She looks directly at Tricia*) I mean ... you just don't know, do you?

This moment

Tricia I've really come to say goodbye.

Cheryl looks at her

They've said I can go today.

Slight moment

Cheryl I thought it was tomorrow you was going.

Tricia They came round and said I can go today. All three of them. The registrar, the houseman *and* Sister. We've made a team decision, Mrs Brinkman, he said. What he means is, they need the bed. So ... (*She smiles*)

Cheryl Good luck to you, girl. (*But she has a sudden thought*) How will you get home?

Tricia They did say they'd arrange a cab for me—but my husband's coming in this afternoon anyway—that's where I've just been—to phone him—or try to, he was out—so—(*she smiles*)—he's going to have something of a surprise when he pops in for his half-hour visit and finds me sitting on the bed with my little suitcase.

Cheryl Nice one, though: nice surprise.

Tricia permits herself a little smile

Tricia Yes. A nice one.

And they are smiling at each other

Cheryl It'll be strange without you.

Tricia It'll be strange not being here.

Cheryl I shall miss our little chats.
Tricia Yes.
Cheryl I really will.
Tricia Me too.
Cheryl I mean we've really got on, haven't we? I mean I suppose it's with us both having the same operation, the same day and that, the way we got on like, but we really have been good mates, haven't we?
Tricia (*smiling*) Good mates, yes.

She instinctively reaches out and takes Cheryl's hand so that they hold hands for a moment and then Cheryl is patting Tricia's hand and letting go of it

Cheryl We won't do none of that soppy stuff about swapping phone numbers, eh? I mean we've had our ... what did you call it ... ?
Tricia (*smiling*) Shared experience.
Cheryl We've had our shared experience and that's where it ends, right? (*She smiles, a little too brightly*)
Tricia Are you all right?
Cheryl Course I am—why?
Tricia I've got to know you, that's all.
Cheryl Know me what?
Tricia Know when there's something on your mind.
Cheryl Just a bit dopey after all that sleep yesterday.

The exchange has not been a heavy one and Cheryl smiles, but Tricia senses that there is something on her mind and Cheryl changes the subject, vaguely indicating the paper she has been holding

I been studying the dinner menu. Again. The amount of pleasure I get deciding where to put my little tick, it's ridiculous. You're missing out on a goodie tonight: moussaka or chicken à la whatsit. (*She smiles, but almost immediately reacts to a sharp pain in her abdomen*)
Tricia Are you all right?

Cheryl nods

Look—I'll go and let you get some sleep.

She makes to stand, but Cheryl stops her

Cheryl (*sudden urgency*) No—no don't go, Trish.

Tricia remains sitting, waiting

See ... I knew you'd be going—well, of course I did—but tomorrow like—and I sort of worked out what I was going to say to you ... not so much say ... just ... talk to you about ... But it's not easy for me, well, you know that, and you going today has thrown me all the more ... I mean, that's great, innit, that's really grown up. (*She smiles, but avoids eye contact*)
Tricia Hey.
Cheryl Sorry.
Tricia And no need for that, either.

Cheryl No. (*And she looks directly at Tricia and even manages a little smile*)

Hazel enters DR. *As before, she neither stops nor looks at them*

Hazel Would you believe no barley sugars? I had to settle for Olde English Mints. (*Holding up the packet*) In those nasty little packets. I said to her if these really *were* Olde English Mints they'd be tipped out of an Olde English Jar into an Olde English Weighing Machine at tuppence a quarter. Went clean over her head, of course, see you later, girls.

Hazel exits L

They watch her go

(*Off*) Now then . . . which of you lot has got their own teeth?

There is a burst of raucous laughter from the unseen women and Cheryl and Tricia find themselves smiling

Tricia I shall miss *her*, I know that.

They continue to smile in this moment

Cheryl It *is* like a club in here, innit? What was it you said . . . a little community, cut off from everything we've ever known and that's right, that's exactly right . . . cut off . . . time to think . . . time to . . . Here, listen to me. But that's what I mean though, see: I think I've said more this past week than I've said in Gawd knows how long. And not only the talking, the listening—listening to some of you girls discussing things—and I mean discussing things—not arguing. I know I haven't joined in a lot—I mean, I know it's been more listening than talking . . . but that's what I shall remember most about being in here: the time to talk and to listen. We never really talk at home, never really discuss things. If we did, I don't know what I'd talk about—at least . . . (*She trails off*) My family are all the same. We never talked about things, never discussed anything— people shouted at each other. Me dad shouted at me mum and me mum shouted at us and we shouted at the kids next door. (*She smiles and gives a little jerk of the head at the thought*) And as for *questioning* things . . . well, you just don't. I mean, not official things. The doctor says, sorry you've got to have your leg off and you say: thanks ever so much, Doctor, when would you like me in? Second opinion? Never heard of it. I didn't even know what I was coming in *here* for, not properly, but then whose fault is that?

Tricia Theirs. They should have explained everything and made sure you understood.

Cheryl (*a little smile*) Yes, well, that's very nice of you, Tricia, but not really. It was down to me. I suppose—I suppose it all comes down to confidence. Being brought up to believe there's nothing you can't do . . . instead of nothing you *can* do. (*There's regret in her voice, but not self-pity. Indeed, there should never be self-pity in anything she says*)

A Male Visitor enters DR. *He holds a bunch of flowers, is clearly unsure of his whereabouts*

His arrival makes Cheryl anxious

That's not the time, is it, it's not visiting already?
Tricia He's twenty minutes early.
Visitor (*to himself*) Where's all the nurses, then?
Tricia (*to the Visitor; friendly*) Can I help you?

The Visitor looks at Tricia

Visitor (*to Cheryl*) I've come to see Mrs Fisher.
Cheryl Mrs Fisher? (*She looks to Tricia*)
Tricia Is she the lady who came in late last night?
Visitor (*to Cheryl*) Mrs Fisher, yes.
Tricia (*pointing*) I think you'll find her in the small ward on the left there.

The Visitor nods absently and moves on, but, as an afterthought, stops

Visitor Thank you.

The Visitor exits UR

Cheryl I didn't know there was anyone new in.
Tricia Heart attack I think.
Cheryl I thought I hadn't seen him before. (*She smiles to herself*) I
remember when I first come in I used to play a sort of game—watching
the visitors coming down the corridor and trying to guess who it was they
was coming to see. You know—from what I'd heard said about them or
from what I'd sort of worked out. (*She smiles*) From what Hazel said I
expected her old man to be covered in hair and chewing on a lump of raw
meat and there he was, this lovely little chap with a smile for everyone and
him and Hazel holding hands and never stopping for breath the whole
time he's here. And I remember imagining *your* husband and gor blimey
what a shock that was—I mean I imagined this great big black fellah, and
there he was ...
Tricia Short white and Jewish. Yes, I know what you mean.

They smile at each other for a moment

Cheryl And see, what's good is that I can say that now—d'you know what I
mean, Tricia, I can *say* things like that now and I know you won't take it
the wrong way like, I mean I know you'll understand.
Tricia (*smiling, and with a slight edge*) Thank you.
Cheryl It's funny though, innit? You get ideas about people even today. I
mean, even today when it's supposed to be all this equality and everything, you can still think, look at her, the toffee-nosed cow. You can still
look at someone or listen to the way they talk and get completely the
wrong end of the stick. (*She smiles to herself at the thought*) My mother
used to call it "stewed prunes and apple tart". Posh people was "stewed
prunes" and common people like us was "apple tart". (*She has pronounced "stewed prunes" with exaggeratedly tight lips and "apple tart"
with exaggeratedly wide mouth*) I mean, you take Gillian there ... (*She
nods in the direction of an unseen woman*) One of the nicest ladies I've ever

met and yet when she first come in I thought, there's a snotty cow, her with her fancy dressing-gown and too stuck up to even say hallo, there's a right plate of stewed prunes and no mistake.

Tricia She was probably just scared. God, I know I was.

Cheryl You? Scared?

Tricia My first time ever in hospital, I was absolutely convinced I was going to die.

Cheryl No.

Tricia I know, it's ridiculous, but it does happen, doesn't it? People go in to have a tooth out and—(*she clicks her fingers*)—that's it.

Cheryl And you seemed so ... I dunno ... so calm.

Tricia God no: sometimes I've wanted a really good cry, a really good scream, sometimes I've really had to force myself to keep control of the situation. (*She knows Cheryl hasn't quite understood this*) Not to give way to stupid fears.

This moment Eileen enters L. *She wears a dressing gown and fluffy slippers, carries her handbag and a newspaper*

Eileen (*to Tricia; a Birmingham accent*) Tell me to mind my own business, I'm a nosy piece I know I am, but did I hear that you're off today, Patricia?

Tricia Yes—yes, I am.

Eileen Yes—well—you look after yourself.

Tricia I will—and you, too.

Eileen (*confidentially to them both*) I've just been having a word with Sister about poor Mrs Maguire ... (*Even more confidential*) They're having trouble finding her veins. And when you think she only came in with her bladder. I said to Sister, I wouldn't be surprised if it wasn't a blood clot, the way she was shouting at that poor woman who brings the tea round. Anyway, I'll leave you to it then, shall I? (*She almost goes, but stops*) I know I tend to butt in sometimes, but it's only my way, I do try to have a chat with everyone but I think we all agree that I never outstay my welcome—don't forget now, Patricia, you look after yourself. (*But she has already spotted an unseen woman*) Oh, there's Cynthia ... I just want to have a quick word with her before they change her dressing. (*And she moves away, pursuing the hastily-departing Cynthia*) Don't forget now, Patricia, you look after yourself ... Cynthia ... I say—Cynthia!

Eileen exits R

Tricia and Cheryl who have not managed to get in more than the odd nod of agreement, watch her go

Tricia I'll bet your first impressions were right about *that* one.

Cheryl No, that one I didn't change my mind about.

And they smile at each other at the thought. A moment

I had completely the wrong idea about *you*, of course. I mean black people just don't talk like you do, not where I come from, anyway. The

truth being, of course, that I've never really *spoken* to a black person so I
mean, you don't *think*, do you, you just ... (*She gropes for the word*)

Tricia Make assumptions. We all do. I certainly do, I'd be a liar if I said
otherwise. I see Tracy in the bed opposite scratching her tattoos and
moving her mouth as she reads the *Sun* and, yes, I make assumptions. It's
whether we're prepared to break those assumptions down. At least we
owe it to each other to try. (*She smiles, without humour, and then frowns
slightly at the memory*) Something very—strange happened the other
night ... the night you were in the observation ward ... the entire night
staff was black. In they marched, these five black nurses—including a new
girl I hadn't seen before—and she came round, this new girl, sort of
letting everyone get to know her, and she was trying very hard, saying
how much she liked the flowers, how pretty someone's hair looked—you
know, trying to make all the right noises ... and somehow something
went wrong. No-one was responding, no-one was—reaching out to her—
and the other black nurses were standing back, watching her and smiling
... and the more anxious she became, the more they smiled, the more
satisfied they were, the more they were enjoying it, and one of them came
over to me and sat on my bed and said "you poor baby darling" and
stroked my brow and I knew that in that moment—and maybe just in that
moment and for no particular reason—those black nurses hated their
white patients and those white women were afraid of those black women,
they felt threatened by them. Next day (*she shrugs, smiles*) it was like it
never happened. (*Slight pause*) Most of the women here are like you,
they've never come into real contact with a black person and have no way
of reading them ... if they're being funny or ironic or friendly or natural
or what ... and the black person becomes offended because she's trying to
communicate, and ... (*She trails off*) I see it all the time but I hoped that
here, in hospital, the differences would somehow become blurred. But
they aren't. Not really. It's just the same.

*There is a burst of noise from the unseen women. They look towards them,
automatically smiling. This moment*

You said you wanted to talk to me about something.

Cheryl No, it's all right, it isn't anything, not really.

Tricia You don't sound very sure.

Cheryl Besides, your husband'll be here in a minute.

Tricia No, he won't be here 'til four.

Cheryl Oh. (*She looks away as though not wanting Tricia to see her
struggling for words*) My husband's coming this afternoon. He's doing
some overtime tonight, so he said he'd ... (*And now she turns back*) Oh
and listen, I'm really grateful for that little chat we had about my son—
that's what I needed, you see—someone to tell me that the way he is is all
right—someone to, what was it, confirm his worth, to agree with me that
he isn't wasting his life.

Tricia (*putting a hand on Cheryl's hand*) Is that it, Cheryl? Is that what you
want to talk about—your son?

For a moment it is as though Cheryl hasn't heard her, but now she is putting her other hand on Tricia's hand and smiling

Cheryl No—no.

The Visitor enters, UR *minus the flowers and moves slowly into the ward taking out a packet of cigarettes. He stands for a moment, looking at the cigarettes and then quickly exits* DR

The two women watch him go

(*Not displeased at changing the subject*) Well that was short and sweet, I must say. I've noticed that, though: it's nearly always the women who stay the longest. Why is it that women seem to have more to say to each other? Course, *they* say, men, that it's just gossiping but it isn't, is it, it's like—I dunno—it's like women seem to *care* more—or at least can show they care, aren't afraid to show they . . . care. (*She trails off, as though embarrassed. Trying to make light of it*) Here, listen to *me*, soppy cow.

And they smile at each other

Tricia I suppose the truth is, men aren't really brought up to care. We want comfort, we go running to Mum. And they certainly don't want to know when something goes wrong with a woman's body, they certainly can't think of us as "patients", as "sick"—they get totally confused—oh, they can make the effort when you're really ill, when you're really bad, but as soon as you're on the mend you can almost hear the impatient shuffling of the feet. I see it all around me. Every visiting hour. Even someone as "enlightened" as Peter, my husband, didn't *really* want to face what was happening to me. (*Which is, of course, her real concern. And now it is her turn to try and make light of it*) Now who's the soppy cow?

And again they smile at each other

Cheryl (*unable to resist*) But—but you're looking forward to going home.
Tricia Oh yes. (*But*) Well, yes and no. I—I think I'm going to find some things hard. Being in here has . . . brought certain things into focus. I know there are things in our lives that will have to change. We don't give enough time to each other, he's obsessed by his work and I think maybe I am too. We don't have enough conversations. We don't——
Cheryl (*suddenly, quickly, as though afraid that if she doesn't say it now she never will*) Trish—I don't want to go home.

This moment

Tricia (*despite herself, trying to make light of it*) I don't think any of us really——
Cheryl I—I don't want to go home.

A moment

Tricia (*gently*) Look, Cheryl—after an operation like you've had—we've had—you're bound to feel——

Cheryl No it isn't that, I mean I know women get depressed and everything after what we've had done, but it's more than that, Trish, it's ... (*She searches for a way to start*) Last time my husband came to see me, he was sitting there where you are and I thought: why are you here, who are we kidding, why don't you go away, we've nothing to say to each other, we've said it all, what there *was* to say, you're only here because it's expected of you. Well I don't expect it anymore, I don't *want* it, so ... I dread him coming here. I do, I dread him coming here. It's like he's—intruding. It's like ... see, Trish, I see him sitting here and I think, I don't love this man, I don't not love him, I don't feel anything for him any more and I know, I know, that he doesn't feel anything for me. He's not a bad man and God only knows he works hard enough. He's never laid a finger on me or the kids. All right, there's been some trouble with Stephen, but I can understand how he feels: he's worked hard all his life and Stephen being like he is ... Look, don't get me wrong, I'm not blaming you or anyone for putting thoughts into my head, but being here, being—*outside* me and him and looking in at what we are and what's left for us ... That lady in the end bed there died and I thought she's gone and in a year from now, maybe less even, it will be like she was never here and it's the same for all of us—unless we ... I don't know what I want, Trish, but I do know that it's more than I've got now, I do know that we can't just—waste—what little time there's been given to us. Not the most earth-shattering thought you've ever heard, except when you wake up sudden in the middle of the night with that terrible knowledge that it's not just a thought, it's *you*. I see him sitting there, past even trying to think of something to say, just—filling up time and I know that inside he's just as ... just as lost as I am but, like me, he's never been able to say it. Well, I'm going to try, this afternoon, when he comes, I'm really going to try, I'm going to try to say all what I've said to you, I'm going to say I know how you feel because I feel it too, and between us ... because we've got to. We've got to.

This moment

Tricia (*gently*) Cheryl ...
Cheryl No, don't say nothing—I just wanted you to listen. (*She attempts a smile*) A rehearsal, like.

A moment

Tricia You see, Cheryl, if it's——
Cheryl No—honest, Trish—don't. I'm just about hanging on as it is.

This moment

Nurse (*off; calling*) Mrs Brinkman?
Tricia (*looking* L) Yes?
Nurse (*off*) Telephone—I think it's your husband.
Tricia Oh—umm—look—could you ask him if he ...
Cheryl Go on—go and speak to him, he'll only get the hump. (*She smiles*)

This moment

Tricia (*to the unseen Nurse*) Coming. (*To Cheryl*) Look, I'll ... If you'll ...
Just ... I'll be back, OK.

This moment

Cheryl (*a little smile; reaching up to touch Tricia's hand*) OK.

*And this moment of them holding hands, smiling at each other and then Tricia
carefully stands and moves away* L

*Eileen passes her, coming the other way. She is holding a small notebook
and ballpoint*

Eileen I thought you'd be gone, Patricia.
Tricia Not yet—sorry.
Eileen No, I'm just saying, I thought you'd be gone. (*And she hasn't stopped
but is already at Cheryl's bedside*)

Tricia exits L, *during the following*

I'll tell you what it is, Cheryl, I've just discovered that it's that nice Nurse
O'Brien's birthday tomorrow and I'm organizing a whip-round to buy
her a little something—I thought fifty p a head, what d'you think? Not
now, I don't want it now, I'm just clearing it in principle so that's all right
then, is it? Good.

*And again, Cheryl has been unable to offer more than the odd nod of
agreement and already Eileen is making a note in her book and moving* UR,
calling after her next victim.

Eileen exits

Cheryl turns to watch her go

Her husband enters DR

*Cheryl turns back to see him standing in the doorway. He holds a newspaper.
This moment. Then he moves to her and kisses her brow perfunctorily*

Husband Hallo.
Cheryl Hallo.
Husband I brought you a paper.
Cheryl That's nice. (*She takes the paper from him*)

*He sits in the chair just vacated by Tricia. There is a burst of laughter from the
unseen women and they both look towards them, with Cheryl again automatically smiling. But then she turns to look at her husband, holding the smile
for him, and he offers one back. Then there is silence between them, which we
hold for as long as possible*

Husband Well, then ... anything to report, is there?

*But he is already taking up the newspaper to look at it and, as he begins to
read, Cheryl looks at him*

A Nurse enters and pulls the curtains across the two upstage beds

The hospital background noises are heard

The Nurse exits L. *Cheryl and her Husband exit*

Waiting

A Nurse, black and professionally cheery, enters, pushing an Old Man in a wheelchair. He wears pyjamas and has a blanket over his legs. He looks very frail—little more than a shell. His eyes are closed

The hospital noises fade and the handbell rings as the Nurse parks the wheelchair downstage

Nurse I'll put you here, shall I—near the window. You can get some sun on your shoulders, you like that, don't you? There, how's that?

He doesn't respond. Not that she expects him to

(*Tidying the blanket*) You just sit here and watch the people. If anyone comes to see you, I'll send them along, all right?

Throughout the following, the Old Man remains unresponsive, eyes closed

She looks at him, gives a little jerk of the head. Fat chance of him getting a visitor. She bends and takes one of his hands

(*Conspiratorially*) I tell you what: when I take you back, we'll go through the gardens. What d'you say, Mr Archer—you and me—a little ride round the gardens, yes?

She continues holding his hand for a moment, then replaces the hand, looks briefly at her watch and exits

A moment. The Lights fade around him. He remains still. Then his eyes open and he smiles as though recognizing someone. He sits forward and his voice will be youthful and firm

Old Man When I was a young boy my mother gave me to understand that I had suffered every complaint under the sun. I remember having yellow jaundice and them putting mustard plasters on me but as I got older I began to have a carefree life and until I was about fourteen years old I was always in some sort of trouble or up to some sort of mischief.

My mum worked in a laundry for thirty years in Kettering Street. There was about five ladies at the ironing benches and four more downstairs at the washing tubs. I was always doing something for fun as I thought, such as getting under the benches while they were ironing and tying strings to the legs of the benches and up to their skirts so that as they went to go into the next room to change the irons, down would come their skirts and show their frilly knickers. They all used to get great laughs out of it and give me sweets every now and again.

He smiles boyishly at the memory. Then reaches under the blanket to take out a Victorian fob watch which he looks at fondly and strokes with his fingers as he speaks

Christmas, we used to play games in the front parlour and Dad did sad monologues. Mum used to cry and we'd all gather round and try to make her laugh. She always used to cry at my dad's monologues, my mum.

A moment

My dad worked for a bookmaker in a running capacity, and me and my sister used to carry the takings to him at the betting club, which was just off Ferry Road near the Angel, as he was half-paralysed down his left side. One very bad Saturday he had been to the barbers when he came out and beckoned me to go across the road. I could see he'd been drinking and I wouldn't go at first, but when I did he had this very thick walking stick which he raised and if he'd caught my head I would have been done for, but instead he caught my shoulder and I was badly bruised.

He was seldom a hasty man, in fact he was very kind-hearted in his own way. It was just that he had a lot of problems. I didn't understand at the time but my mother, who was very gentle, used to explain things to me.

A moment. Then he is suddenly staring at the watch without really seeing it

Here, look at the time, come on, you lot, he'll be home soon . . . Where's that jug? Albert—go and cadge a drop of milk off Mrs Hinson . . . Look at the time . . . look at the time . . .

He stuffs the watch back under the blanket and seems very agitated, looking around as though expecting to see someone he doesn't want to see. He calms. A moment

When I left school, I went to work with this German firm in Tunhill Row. The only thing I was any good at was carpentry and my dad got me in with them because they was cabinet-makers. He was a funny old man, this German. He had a very old piece of mahogany which every now and again he used to cut into and hold up for me to smell the richness of it.

He brings his hands to his mouth as though smelling the wood

He taught me to carve and they put me on to restoring mirrors.

When the war came, me and my brother got put in the same mob. When we got to France they shoved us right up front. I got some gas and they sent me to Number Four General Hospital because of my stomach. I went back and got a bit of shrapnel so they put me on a boat to Folkestone. I went back to the old firm but there'd been some trouble and they shut it down. There wasn't much call for my kind of work so I got a job as a packer.

My brother—young Georgie—got killed on the very last day of the war. He was my father's favourite, young George. I mean no-one said anything but you could tell. Sometimes my father used to look at me and . . .

A look of hatred comes into his face. Then he pulls out the watch

(*Almost a shout*) I'm just going down the corner! You heard me. It's my
money and I'll spend it how I soddin' like ... The day you're starving is
the day you can complain ... Look at the time ... look at the bloody
time ...

He sinks back into the chair. A moment

I met my Florrie in a pub near the Angel. She had on a coat with a big fur
collar—I remember because the tar was melting in the streets. We was
walking out together for about six months and then a mate of mine sold
me this ring and I showed it to her and said, how about it, and she said,
you're a bit pleased with yourself, aren't you, but I don't suppose I'll do
no better, so we got married down Saint Mark's and moved into the
buildings down Popham Street. We had five in all but the three girls died
in the 'flu and Arthur got taken by the Japs in Singapore. Billy done very
well for himself and got in at the grammar school. His youngest is thirty
now. They live—up north somewhere.

*A moment. Then he begins to sing the old Paul Robeson lullaby. Quietly at
first, but building gently*

> "Lu-la lu-la lu-la lu-la bye-byes
> Do you want the moon to play with?
> Or the stars to run away with?
> They'll come if you don't cry ..."

He stops part-way through and then continues speaking

Florrie used to laugh at me because of my ambition. I had a good voice, I
did. People used to come down the *Half Moon* of a Friday just to hear the
pleasure of it. She had no right to throw my stuff away like that. She was
jealous, that was her trouble. When I done that show, I know just what
she was thinking, she was jealous.

We would have stayed in the buildings, you know. Didn't want to know
nothing about no re-housing. Foreign he was, our landlord. Never seen
him. This bloke come round. From the council, with this letter. What's
this, I said? They're all coming down, he said, the whole street, you're
being re-housed. We're staying where we bleeding are, mate, I said.

She was a fine-looking woman, my Florrie. Right into her fifties. I've got
some lovely photos of her. In my box. Where's my box, have you seen my
box?

He looks around hopelessly for his box

Mind you, I had a lot of trouble with her when we was walking out. All
these clever young mashers tilting their hats and making eyes as though I
couldn't see. Fancy her going like that. I come home from work and she
was sitting in a chair like she had no life in her. The doctor came and said
it was a virus. In her kidneys, I think he said. Never been ill in her life, she
hadn't. Three weeks and ... she just went.

A moment. And he begins to sing

> The woman next door to me
> The woman next door to me
> She's the happiness of my life
> I like her much better than my old woman
> Though she's all right
> As right as right can be
> But I could spend a better half-hour
> With the woman next door to me.

He has started off firmly, but the last two lines have trailed away. He looks anxiously at the watch

I must go, Josie, I must go, look at the time.

He shoves the watch back under the blanket and looks around angrily

If she's not back here in ten minutes, I'll kill her, I will, I'll bloody kill her. Oil of wintergreen, you just try it . . . plenty of time . . . plenty of time . . .

And his speech continues, rambling, varied in pitch and pace

I should have gone, I should have tried, I know I should . . . but there was them to think about, you just can't walk out on a family, you just can't turn your back and . . . children . . . flesh and blood . . . you just can't . . .

And now his ramblings are mingled with the recorded sounds of his own voice

Voice Watch it, look out, copper coming!
Old Man She laughed . . . she had no right to laugh . . .
Voice I'll tell your father, you see if I don't . . .
Old Man . . . yes, sir, just for the weekend, sir . . . start Monday . . .
Voice Not again, oh Christ not again . . . look at my soddin' boots, sod the bleeding froggies . . .
Old Man What queue? Waddya mean wrong queue? I been standing here gone half an hour . . . I don't *want* no stamps . . .
Voice . . . I shall want to pay for my keep . . .
Old Man . . . there'll be no question about me not paying for my keep . . .
Voice . . . where's Dolly? What's the time?
Old Man It's flesh and blood, see Josie . . .
Voice Flesh and blood . . .
Old Man I can't just turn my back on them . . .
Voice Flesh and blood . . . flesh and blood . . .
Old Man I was a good tradesman . . . a *craftsman* I was . . . people used to *watch* me . . . watch my hands . . .

He stares down at his clenched and shaking hands

Can't just . . .

He puts his hands to his mouth as though smelling something

Voice A thousand years growing . . . some respect we must give . . .

Old Man What's the time?

He fumbles for his watch

Christ. Christ!

He holds the watch out at arm's length towards the audience as though desperately offering it for someone to take

(*Scarcely audible*) Mama.

His arm slowly lowers. His eyes slowly close. The Lights around him dim and slowly fade as the hospital background noises fade up

A Nurse enters and wheels the Old Man off UR

A second Nurse enters L, *pushing a telephone trolley which she wheels to stand downstage of the* DR *bed. Sandra enters and gets on to the* DR *bed*

Magic

The Lights change as the Nurse pulls back the curtains to reveal the two upstage beds

May is in the UR *bed, and her husband, Arthur, sits in the chair* R *of the bed. Brenda is in the* UL *bed. Sandra lies on top of the* DR *bed*

The Nurse exits L

May is a working-class pensioner and is reading the "TV Times". Arthur wears a cap, scarf and raincoat and reads the "Sun". They make no effort at conversation—their silence is not strained. On the bedside cabinet is a vase containing a few dying blooms

Brenda is in her mid-thirties. She wears a knitted bedjacket and a set of headphones, and is reading a magazine. There is a large get-well card and a box of chocolates on her cabinet. The visitor's chair is R *of the bed*

Sandra is black and in her early twenties. She is wearing pyjamas and a short dressing-gown, and has a cheerful ribbon in her hair. She is using the portable telephone downstage of the bed and is whispering flirtatious conversation with her boyfriend. On the cabinet upstage of the bed are a vase holding six long-stemmed red roses, and a small pile of tenpence pieces for the phone. There is no bedside chair

We hold this scene for a moment and then the handbell rings and the hospital noises fade

Ron enters UR

Ron (*nodding all round to the patients*) Good-evening.

Joan enters behind him and sees Brenda

Joan There she is!

Ron turns

Here she is!

Joan and Ron are middle-aged and wear evening dress. Joan has a fur stole over her dress. Ron wears a white dinner jacket

Sandra is completely involved in her telephone conversation and is oblivious to their arrival. May and Arthur look up from their reading and unashamedly look and listen to the following

Brenda (*clearly not expecting visitors; pulling off the headphones*) Oh. Hallo, Joan.
Joan Told you she'd be surprised, didn't I?
Ron (*pointedly, to Brenda*) How d'you do.
Joan Sorry. *Sorry.* This is my husband, Ronald.
Ron (*shaking Brenda's hand*) Pleased to meet you. Didn't we bump into each other at the firm's dinner dance?
Brenda I didn't go to the firm's dinner dance.
Ron Are you sure?
Joan Brenda doesn't involve herself in functions.

Joan gives Ron a meaningful look and indicates for him to help her off with the stole, which he does. Joan indicates her ornate dress, involving the watching May and Arthur

Don't mind this . . . Ladies Night at The Lodge.

Joan sits in the chair, careful of her dress, and Ron arranges the stole carefully over the back of the chair

Why didn't you *say* you were being hospitalized?
Brenda You were on holiday.
Ron Don't talk about our holiday, Brenda—please.

Ron nudges Joan and they giggle, involving the watching May and Arthur. Brenda tries to join in with a faint smile. They all turn to regard Sandra as she speaks

Sandra (*urgently*) No, it's all right, I've got some more money—hold on . . . (*She grabs the tenpence pieces and pushes one into the box*) Hallo? Barry? (*She smiles, relieved, and continues her private conversation*)
Joan How are you getting on with the other patients? (*She clearly means Sandra*)
Brenda Oh, it's lovely really. Everyone's really nice. Really friendly.
Joan Jolly good. (*Giving Ron one of her looks*) Anyway. I'd just taken some dictation for Mr Broadley—who is still behaving like a pig by the way, the sooner he leaves that poor wife of his the better, we all know what's going on, I don't know who he thinks he's kidding—when it suddenly occurred to me: where is our Brenda, I said. She's in hospital, she said. Sharon. His—you know. I don't know how she's got the cheek to hold her head up in that office, let alone pass out information.
Brenda They sent me a lovely card.

During the following, Ron takes up the card, briefly reads it and returns it to the cabinet. He then wanders; unhooks the chart at the bottom of Sandra's bed, looks at it, looks at her, and replaces it. Sandra is deep in phone-talk and does not acknowledge any of this

Joan Yes. They said.
Brenda And a beautiful box of chocolates. Handmade.
Joan Have any of them been to see you?
Brenda Not yet—no.
Joan (*a meaningful look to May and Arthur*) No.
Brenda I expect they'll come later—you know—afterwards.
Joan (*taking Brenda's hand*) Do you know this girl's got no family.
Ron (*absently, reading Sandra's chart*) That's a bit of bad.
Brenda I have got a sister, actually.
Joan Not a sister you can talk to.

Joan has included May and Arthur in this information, so that Brenda is now aware of them

Brenda We had a disagreement.
Joan When did you last speak?
Brenda These things go on, don't they?

During the following, the others all turn and listen to Sandra, who is totally unaware of them

Sandra What? ... I *can't* ... No ... *No*, Barry ... (*She smiles coyly*) Because people can hear, that's why. ... No, I *won't* say it. Not even for you. Oh look, now look what you've done, you've made me blush, you're wicked, you are. ... Because I'm not talking dirty when people can hear, not even for you, Barry Winters. ... Yes, I know I did but that was different, I was on the switchboard.

When it is clear that there is nothing more to listen to, Joan pats Brenda's hand comfortingly and Ron perches on the edge of the bed, careful of his trouser creases

Joan Anyway, I said to Ronald, that girl will need cheering up, I said. What we'll do is pop by on our way out.
Sandra What? ... Of course I like it. You know I like it.

Again, the others are looking and listening. Arthur cranes forward

(*Smiling; even more coy*) Oh all right then—just this once—and I'm not repeating it so you'd better listen ...

Arthur shows his disappointment when Sandra cups the receiver, turning away, so that they can't hear

Joan And I'll tell you something else, Brenda—when it comes to cheering people up, you don't have to look much further than my Ronald.
Ron (*standing, posing*) Da-da! (*He moves round the bed so that he is in full view*)

Joan He does a turn.

May nudges Arthur violently

Brenda Oh yes?

Brenda looks somewhat anxiously at Ron who does a little soft-shoe shuffle. May nudges Arthur again and whispers in his ear

Joan And I've no doubt he'll be called upon to do one tonight.
Ron (*generally*) They get somewhat raucous, these Lodge Nights.
Joan (*to Ron, prompting*) So . . . we may not have brought . . .
Ron (*responding quickly; pushing back his cuffs*) So . . . we may not have brought any handmade chocolates, but what we——
May I say.

They turn to regard her

Excuse me, my hubbie and I was wondering, would we by any chance have seen you on the telly?
Joan (*sighing heavily*) We get this all the time.

She beams proudly at Ron who is suddenly very modest

May You're not that singer, are you? You're not that Scotland's answer to Des O'Connor?
Ron No, no—strictly amateur.
Arthur There you are, you see—I told you his legs was longer.
May That's our set. I keep telling him, it's our set.
Joan Actually—he has had offers to go legit as they say, but we talked it over and decided against.
Ron It's a closed shop, anyway. Who you know, Magic Circle, all that stuff.
Arthur Don't talk to me about closed shops.
May My hubbie was with London Transport for thirty years.
Ron That's handy.
May He could tell you stories that would stop you boarding a bus for the rest of your life.
Joan Actually, we're not desperately into public transport—not with Ronald's petrol allowance and the garage being virtually *en suite.*
Sandra (*suddenly alert*) Barry? Who's that? Have you got someone with you? Who have you got there? . . . Don't lie to me, Barry, I can hear someone laughing . . . (*She quickly feeds a coin into the box, fumbling*) Barry . . . Barry? . . .

The money has gone in too late and she has to re-dial. She does so, and will do so several times, the call not being answered, throughout the following

Joan (*pointedly*) You were saying, Ronald.

A moment as he drags his eyes away from Sandra

Ron (*brightly*) So . . . we may not have brought any handmade chocolates, but what we did bring—what we *did* bring . . . was . . . some fruit! (*And suddenly he produces an orange*)

Ron shows the orange all round and then tosses it to Arthur, who, during the following, stares at it as though checking its authenticity. Humming his working tune, Ron produces various items of fruit from various places: a bunch of grapes from behind a pillow, a banana from up his sleeve, a wicker fruit-basket from the inside tail of his coat, and—with lewd suspense—a cucumber from under the bedclothes. Each of these items is passed to Joan, who, like the magician's assistant, exhibits each in turn before it goes into the basket which finally goes on top of the cabinet. Arthur retains the orange, and, throughout the following, spreads his handkerchief like a small tablecloth, takes out a penknife, peels, sections and chews the orange somewhat toothlessly

Sandra (*pressing money into the box*) Barry? Why did you take so long to answer, what were you doing? . . . Oh don't come that, you knew it was me and there *was* someone there, I know there was—what's going on, Barry—why aren't you here like you promised?

The others wait a moment for the outcome, but none seems forthcoming

Joan He does jokes as well.
Brenda Oh. (*She attempts a smile but is more concerned about what the other occupants of the ward may be thinking about this demonstration*)
Ron Actually, there's not a lot you can teach me about hospitals, my father was a doctor.

Joan plumps the pillows so that Brenda is unwillingly leaning forward

Joan You have to join in.
Brenda Sorry?
Joan You have to feed him.
Ron About hospitals. My father was a doctor.
May I say . . . (*She leans forward and mouths the words: "your father was a doctor?" whilst indicating for Brenda to say it*)
Brenda Your father was a doctor?
Ron That is correct . . . a bus condoctor! Move along there, room for one more inside!

He pretends to get into bed alongside Brenda, much to Joan's merriment

Joan You're shocking, you are! (*To May and Arthur*) He's shocking, he is!
Ron And now, ladies, since I have nowhere to sit, I shall exit stage left and conjure up a chair.

He produces a large plum from Brenda's nose, shows it, and passes it to Joan, who puts it in the fruit basket

Ron exits L, cheerfully

Joan Never a dull moment.
Brenda No.
May I say . . .

Joan and Brenda regard her

. . . we met Yul Brynner once. In a lay-by on the A10. We were visiting my sister and my hubbie got taken short.

Sandra What? I never *said* that, Barry. You've got no right saying I said that, why would I have said that? ... No, you haven't Barry, not after all I've done for you, why are you doing this to me?

The others listen in the hope of finding out

Joan (*confidentially*) What is it—the scrape or the big one?
Brenda Ummm ... the big one.

Joan dramatically sucks in air

Joan I had the scrape, you know, and that was bad enough.
Brenda He said it will be more uncomfortable than anything.
Joan Who did?
Brenda The specialist.
Joan Yes, well ... specialists.
May I say. *I'm* internal, you know.
Joan (*sniffily*) Oh yes?
May Yes. I was internal before an' all.
Joan Yes—it's usually internal with a woman.
May I should imagine ninety per cent of this ward is internal.
Arthur Pain isn't a patch on what it was in my day. Now we *did* suffer.
Sandra *What*? ... I don't believe this is happening to me, Barry. I really don't believe this is happening.
Joan (*her face brightening*) Here he comes!

Ron enters R, *bringing a chair which he sets at the bedside*

Ron I just bumped into a friend of mine, actually. He was downstairs, giving a urine sample. (*Miming holding a glass*) The doctor said to him: Do you know, your urine is ninety-nine per cent alcohol. Good God, Doctor, he said, why is that? I've no idea, said the doctor ... cheers! (*He mimes toasting and drinking and sits*)
Joan You are, you're shocking! He is, isn't he, shocking!
Ron (*to Arthur*) Another friend of mine, just had an operation for——
Joan Stop it, stop it!

Joan and Ron cease their merriment and settle

Sandra Barry! Don't you hang up on me, Barry. Don't you dare hang up on ... (*But clearly he hangs up on her. She takes her last coin and re-dials and inserts the coin during the following*)
Joan (*serious, confidential; of Brenda*) She's having the B-I-G-O-N-E.

Ron frowns, not understanding

May I say.

Ron looks at her

The Big One.
Ron Ah!
Joan (*heavily*) The specialist told her it would be more uncomfortable than anything.

Ron Had a chat with you yet, has he, Brenda? The surgeon? Told you exactly what they're going to do, has he?
Brenda No.
Ron Oh.

Slight pause

Brenda Is that bad?
All No, no, no, no . . .
Ron It's just that they generally have a little chat with you, that's all.
Brenda Well, he hasn't.
May I say. I expect he'll do it nearer the time.
Joan Just what I was about to say, thank you.
Brenda There's no reason why he shouldn't really, is there?
Ron ⎫
Joan ⎭ *(together)* Course there isn't.

Slight pause

Ron Only if there's any complications——
Joan *Ronald!*
Ron Forget I said that.
Joan Too late now. *(She takes Brenda's hand)* The only time they don't tell you what they're going to do is if there are any complications.
Ron They don't want you to worry, you see.
Brenda But I haven't got any complications.
Joan Of course you haven't.
Brenda They would have said by now.
Joan Course they would. *(She looks closer at Brenda's hand, then sets it down delicately as though it might be diseased)*
May I say. Sometimes they prefer to break it to the next-of-kin.
Joan Unfortunately, she hasn't got any next-of-kin.
Brenda I've got a sister.
Joan Did you tell them?
Brenda They didn't ask.
Ron Well then. That's it. *(He pats her stomach)* No problem.
Brenda Actually . . . I don't like talking about it.

They fall into silence and listen to the following

Sandra Why? Because you live in my flat and pay not one penny towards it, that's why, Barry. Because I go out to work every day leaving you lying in bed reading the *NME* and upsetting the neighbours with your amplifiers, that's why, Barry. Because you're the father of my child—that's also why, Barry. Now these things may not mean a lot to you, but to me they're rather important and they're just some of the reasons—not all of them, Barry, just some of them—why I think you should reconsider what you've just said to me. . . . No, it isn't a question of nagging, Barry, it's a question of human rights . . . Barry? . . . *Barry!*

Now, and as though to reassure herself more than anything

Brenda I think doctors are wonderful.

The others join in enthusiastically, overlapping almost

Joan And nurses.
Ron Nurses . . . porters.
May Tea ladies.
Arthur Ambulance drivers.
Joan Radiographers.
Ron Forensic scientists.
May That woman in the paper shop.
Arthur Ambulance drivers.
Brenda Everyone, really.
May Mind you, they're born to it, aren't they?
Joan Who are?
May Medical people.
Joan *Medical* people—oh yes.
Ron And when you think what they're paid.
Joan And they wonder why the National Health is coming apart at the seams.
Ron You cannot deny it, Brenda: money—talks! (*And he produces a tenpenny piece from Brenda's mouth—shows it round—and is about to pocket it*)
Sandra (*an edge of desperation*) Excuse me—is that a ten p? Can I borrow it please?
Ron Oh—yes—certainly.

Ron moves across and, under Joan's beady stare, gives the coin to Sandra who almost snatches it from him and inserts it into the box and dials as Ron is about to move back but sees Arthur methodically quartering the orange

Joan What you mustn't do is let yourself get depressed.
Brenda I'm not.
Ron (*pointing*) Excuse me, is that my orange?
Arthur Yes—yes it is.
Ron He's eating my orange.
May Don't make so much noise when you eat. I say . . . the thing is, he's got no mastication. My sister was just the same. She lost her teeth immediately prior to losing her hubbie.
Sandra (*angrily*) Barry—why did you do that? Don't you ever dare put the phone down on me again—don't you ever dare . . . (*But he has obviously put the phone down. To Arthur*) Excuse me—you haven't by any chance got any ten p's, have you? I'll pay you back, thankseversomuch.
Arthur Let's see what we've got, shall we? (*He finds her some tenpence pieces*)
Joan They'll probably let you have some pills if you ask. It can be very depressing lying in bed all day, *I* know. (*To Ron*) Do you remember how Vera was after she had her big one? Took her months before she could bring herself to so much as boil an egg.

Ron I don't wish to diminish your condition, Brenda, but what you're having done is bread and butter to these people.

Joan They must do about a dozen a week.

Ron And how often do you hear of any mishap?

Joan Never.

Pause

Not if we don't count your uncle Leslie.

Ron Not the same though, is it, Joannie?

Joan It *was* major surgery, Ronald—and that *is* what we are discussing when we're not ingratiating ourselves with perfect strangers, surely?

Ron True enough, I suppose.

Pause. Sandra's caller hangs up

May I say. What happened to his uncle Leslie?

Ron They never found out.

Joan Went in to have a cyst removed and died on the table.

Ron Strong as an ox he was.

Joan There was an inquiry of course.

Ron Fat lot of use that was.

Joan Have you ever tried sueing a doctor?

Ron (*to Brenda*) If anything goes wrong, don't bother.

Joan Closing ranks isn't in it.

Ron Look at Mrs Harbold at number sixty-eight.

Joan Sewed her up with a pair of scissors inside her—and who gets the blame? The porter who wheeled her in.

Ron Mind you. She's made a miraculous recovery.

Joan The way she manoeuvres that chair of hers. She is, she is a living legend.

Sandra's caller hangs up

Arthur Don't talk to *me* about medical technology: my father never took a pill in his entire life and still he died with a full head of hair.

May Mind you, he always *was* vain.

Arthur My mother took him in a cup of tea, went back half an hour later, the tea was stone-cold and so was he.

A moment

Brenda You didn't have a very good holiday, then.

Ron Oh? What makes you say that, Brenda?

Brenda You said you didn't want to talk about it.

Ron We had a wonderful holiday—wonderful.

Joan It's just that it was so full of laughs that when we talk about it we can't help re-living it and getting a fit of the giggles. What about that couple on the surfboard, I didn't know where to put my face.

Ron Neither did he by the look of it!

Joan and Ron laugh merrily, involving May and Arthur. Sandra's caller hangs up

Joan Tell her about the—you know. (*She mouths and mimes to Ron behind her hand*)

Ron Oh—yes!

Joan (*generally*) You'll like this.

Ron On the way back—chappie comes up to me at the airport—holding this box. (*He indicates about shoebox size*) Asks me if I wouldn't mind taking it back to London for him. What's in it, I said. He takes the lid off and shows me—it's a human eye, sitting on a bed of cotton wool. Apparently, he's from the local hospital and the eye is needed urgently for a transplant at St Thomas's. I was only too happy to oblige of course. Any special instructions during transit, I said. Yes, he said, make sure it gets a seat near the window!

Joan has been mouthing the last part of this story with him, desperate for him to get to the punchline and now they laugh merrily, prodding Brenda. May and Arthur remain stone-faced as ever. A moment as Joan and Ron calm down, and then they all realize that Sandra is crying, dialling through her tears

Sandra Operator . . . I wonder if you can help me. I keep getting cut off and I know there's someone there because I've been speaking to them. . . . Yes. . . . Yes. . . . Thank you . . .

This moment

Joan Did they say anything about convalescence?

Brenda They said I wouldn't be able to work for a bit.

Joan It's usually about three months.

Brenda Nine weeks they said.

Joan No, no—to be safe—three months minimum.

Ron Look what happened to you-know-who.

Joan You have to be so very careful. Put your feet up, no lifting, take things very very easily. Otherwise . . . (*She sucks in air*)

May I say. She'll have to leave it all to her hubbie.

Joan (*heavily*) She hasn't got a husband.

Ron Boyfriend then—eh, Brenda?

Joan She doesn't *mix*.

Brenda I'm sure I can manage, thank you.

Joan Course you will.

Ron Course you will.

Joan (*an aside to May*) Mind you, that's what Vera said.

Sandra Thank you, Operator. . . . Yes, I'll try again later. Thank you.

She replaces the receiver. She seems to have regained her composure. She sees the others looking at her, smiles, gets up from the bed, takes up her purse and digs into it and holds out a coin for Arthur to take

Five times ten is fifty p, right? Thanks for your help. (*She smiles generally, then turns, takes up the vase of roses and—with no warning of what she is about to do—tips them into the wastebin shouting*) You shit! You bastard! We're finished—can you hear me, Barry Winters—*finished!* (*And she hobbles away—walking from the knees down so as not to disturb her stitches, knees together*) Finished, you bastard . . . finished!

All heads are turned in unison to watch her departure

Sandra exits L, *but can still be heard shouting abuse at her Barry*

The shouts die away. Silence for a moment

Joan I expect what you're worried about more than anything is losing your femininity.
Brenda How d'you mean, losing my femininity?

But she is more concerned about Sandra than anything else and constantly looks in the direction of her departure as Joan speaks

Joan That's usually what happens to women when they have The Big One, wouldn't you say, Ronald?
Ron It does seem to be psychologically damaging, I must say.
Brenda How d'you mean—psychologically damaging?
Joan Not being able to have any more children—or in your case, to have any children at all.
Ron Combined with the belief that you are no longer desirable to the opposite S-E-X.
Joan Or indeed, whether it is possible for you to continue having a S-E-X-ual relationship—or, in your case, begin one.
Brenda (*of Sandra*) Shouldn't someone see if she's all right?
Joan I think you'll find they have trained staff for that sort of thing. Besides . . . (*She lets the "besides" hang heavy with implication*)
May (*nudging Arthur*) Do you remember what that specialist said to our Maureen . . . (*To the others*) I say, I was saying what this specialist said to our Maureen when she had *her* Big One.
Joan (*tartly*) Oh yes?
May She was worried about *her* maritals—her Stanley being an animal and unsaturated, especially when the drink was on him—anyway, do you know what he said, this specialist, the saucy devil?

A moment as she waits for a response

Ron No?
May He said, don't you worry, Mrs Tooley, he said, we shall be taking away the baby carriage but we shall be leaving the playpen.

Ron enjoys this, unaware of Joan's beady annoyance. Brenda is still looking anxiously after Sandra

Ron (*taking out a small notebook*) Oh yes—that's a good one—I shall just jot that one down if I may.
May By all means, dear—you never know when these things come in handy, do you?

But Ron becomes aware of Joan's beady look and discreetly pockets the book during the following

Joan Luckily though, in Brenda's case, these considerations don't apply.

Ron How's that, Joannie?
Joan Brenda not being married.
Ron Ah.
Joan Or any prospect of it.
Ron You can't be sure.
Joan I think we can in Brenda's case. (*She pats Brenda's hand. Brightly*)
You don't think about it, do you, Brenda?
Brenda Don't think about what?
Joan The fact that you'll never have any children.
Brenda No, I don't, actually.
Joan No, of course you don't.
Ron Of course, for a lot of women it's their entire *raison d'être*.
May (*nudging Arthur sharply*) Haven't I always said it?
Joan Look at Sylvia at number twelve. (*She takes out her compact and checks her make-up during the following*)
Arthur What about her?
Ron Just sits. Staring out of the window.
May Oh I say.
Joan She was so vivacious, so alive.
Ron Tried to kill herself again last week, you know.
Joan *No!*
Ron Yes—he told me. She's tried it again, Ron, he said.
Joan What was it—the pills again?
Ron No, no—tried to hang herself.
May Oh I say.
Brenda Excuse me. I really do think someone should see if she's all right.

And without fuss, Brenda gets up and briskly exits L

The others watch her go. A moment

Ron She's a funny one, Joannie.
Joan I told you, didn't I?
May (*levering herself out of bed*) If you'll excuse me, I just want to avail myself of the toilet.

May exits L *as quickly as she can, clearly wanting to be in on whatever's going on*

When she has gone, Arthur unhurriedly moves to Sandra's bed, retrieves the roses from the bin, moves back, jettisons the weary blooms from May's vase and replaces them with the roses, topping up the water from Brenda's jug. This as Joan takes up Brenda's box of chocolates and inspects them

Joan Hand-made chocolates, my foot.
Ron Any going spare, are there?

He sorts himself out a chocolate as Joan looks inside the get-well card

Joan Just as I thought. Mr Broadley's signature—forged.

She triumphantly shows the card round and sneaks a chocolate. Ron sits, feet up, on Brenda's bed and will take out a pack of cards to practise some sleight of hand as the telephone by Sandra's bed rings. Joan moves across and takes it up briskly and efficiently

Hallo? ... No she's not available at the moment—is that Barry by any chance? ... (*She sits on Sandra's bed and becomes involved in the phone*) No—not at all—just *en passant* as they say, but quite fortunate as it happens because it does give me the opportunity to fill you in as it were. Now far be it from me to interfere, Barry, but in my opinion, your young lady is, shall we say, slightly unstable. ... Yes. ... (*And she continues her conversation swinging her legs up on to the bed during the following*)
Arthur I say.

Ron turns to him

Bloke goes into the Intensive Care Ward and there, lying on the bed in the corner, is this head. Just the head. So he goes up to it and he says, good-morning, and the head says, sod off out of it. So he goes to his doctor, this bloke, and he says, that is fantastic, that head there in the corner. Yes, it's all we could save of him, says the doctor, it's quite an achievement, he should, of course, be dead. Then why is he so miserable, says the bloke. Ah well, says the doctor, we've just told him he's got to have all his teeth out. (*He waits for a response*)
Ron I don't get it.
Joan (*cupping the receiver*) I don't think that's very nice, do you, Ronald? (*And she goes back to her phone talking*)
Arthur It's this head, you see.
Ron Yes, I know that, I just don't get it.
Arthur There's this bloke, you see.
Ron Yes?
Arthur He goes into this Intensive Care Unit ...

He continues trying to explain his joke to the humourless Ron, while at the same time taking up another piece of Brenda's fruit and peeling it

Ron (*shuffling his cards and offering them to Arthur*) Choose a card.

So that each of them now has a bed: Ron listening to Arthur's explanation of his joke and doing his card trick at the same time; Arthur explaining the joke, peeling the fruit and trying to remember which card he took; Joan giving advice on the telephone to Barry. And the hospital noises fade in and get louder and louder as the Lights fade to Black-out

CURTAIN

FURNITURE AND PROPERTY LIST

ACT I

On stage: Three hospital beds with bedclothes. *Above each:* temperature chart, radio headphones, oxygen outlet
Three hospital bedside cabinets. *On top of each:* jug of water, box of tissues. *On top of* UR *cabinet*: **Eric**'s spectacles
Three chairs
Bed tray at foot of UL bed
Waste-bin by side of DR bed
Curtain rail with curtains (pulled around UR bed)

Off stage: Basket containing bowl, spoon, Thermos flask of soup, gingham tablecloth, plate, spoon, trifle in a plastic box **(Helen)**
Large bag **(Pauline)**
Large mirror, clipboard, stick mike **(Fiona)**
Sound and practical camera lighting equipment, make-up box with make-up **(Julia)**
Small ENG camera **(Maureen)**
Telephone **(Naomi)**
Newspaper **(Woman)**
Newspaper **(2nd Woman)**

Personal: **Helen:** handbag containing handkerchief
Pauline: wedding ring on finger, wet umbrella
Fiona: wrist-watch
Darbon: tubes connected to instruments
Maureen: wrist-watch
Mother: spectacles
Critic: horn-rimmed spectacles

ACT II

On stage: Three hospital beds with bedclothes. *Above each*: temperature chart, radio headphones, oxygen outlet
Three hospital bedside cabinets. *On each*: jug of water, box of tissues.
Visitor's chair R of UL bed
Visitor's chair R of UR bed
Curtain rail with curtains (pulled back)
Piece of paper (for **Cheryl**)

Off stage: Packet of mints **(Hazel)**
Bunch of flowers **(Visitor)**
Newspaper **(Eileen)**
Small notebook and pen **(Eileen)**

> Newspaper **(Husband)**
> Wheelchair **(Nurse)**

Personal: **Hazel:** handbag, catheter bag
         Visitor: packet of cigarettes
         Eileen: handbag
         Nurse: watch
         Old Man: Victorian fob watch

When the lighting dims (Page 44)

Set: Vase of dying flowers on UR bedside cabinet
    Large get-well card and box of chocolates on UL bedside cabinet
    Vase of six long-stemmed red roses, pile of tenpence pieces, purse
      containing fifty pence piece on DR bedside cabinet
    Copy of *TV Times* (for **May**)
    Copy of the *Sun* (for **Arthur**)
    Magazine (for **Brenda**)
    UL *bed*: bunch of grapes behind pillow, cucumber under bedclothes,
      hidden wicker fruit-basket

Off stage: Telephone trolley **(Nurse)**
      Chair **(Ron)**

Personal: **Arthur:** handkerchief, penknife, five tenpence pieces
      Ron: orange, banana, large plum, tenpence piece, small notebook and pen,
        pack of playing cards
      Joan: handbag containing mirror compact

LIGHTING PLOT

Property fittings required: nil

Interior. The same scene throughout

ACT I

To open: General half-light

Cue 1	A **Nurse** enters UR *Bring up lighting on* UR *bed*	(Page 1)
Cue 2	The **Nurse** pulls the curtains around the UR bed *Crossfade to lighting on* DR *bed*	(Page 8)
Cue 3	**Pauline:** "I would have been here earlier ..." *Start slow fade to Black-out*	(Page 14)
Cue 4	**Fiona:** "... St Leonard's hospital, May fifteenth." *Snap on spot on* **Fiona**	(Page 15)
Cue 5	**Fiona:** "... leading transplant surgeons." *Snap off spot on* **Fiona** *and snap on spot on* **Naomi**	(Page 15)
Cue 6	**Naomi:** "Hallo." *Black-out*	(Page 15)
Cue 7	**Fiona:** "Super." *Bring up lighting on* **Naomi, Fiona, Julia** *and* **Maureen**	(Page 15)
Cue 8	**Julia:** "Are these theirs or wardrobe?" *Black-out; then bring up lighting on* UL *bed*	(Page 16)
Cue 9	**Nurse:** "... he's lining up a quadruple." *Snap on spot on* **Naomi**	(Page 23)
Cue 10	**Naomi:** "He's bloody *what*?" *Snap off spot*	(Page 23)
Cue 11	**Nurse:** "first with the quadruple." *Snap on spot on* **Woman**	(Page 23)
Cue 12	**Woman:** " '... Top Surgeon Speaks.' " *Snap on spot on* **2nd Woman**	(Page 23)
Cue 13	**2nd Woman:** " '... Midnight Mercy Dash.' " *Snap off two spots*	(Page 23)
Cue 14	**Fiona:** "Yesterday." *Snap on spots on* **Mother** *and* **Father**	(Page 24)
Cue 15	**Fiona** (voice over): "Cut!" *Snap off spots on* **Mother** *and* **Father**	(Page 24)

Cue 16	**Naomi:** "... speak to his daughter and her husband." *Snap on spots on* **Son-in-law** *and* **Daughter**	(Page 25)
Cue 17	**Son-in-law:** "... wasn't his body anyway." *Snap off spots on* **Son-in-law** *and* **Daughter**	(Page 25)
Cue 18	**Fiona:** "... a complete waste of time?" *Snap on spot on* **Naomi**	(Page 26)
Cue 19	**Naomi:** "Can we go again please?" *Snap off spot on* **Naomi** *and snap on spot on* **Critic**	(Page 26)
Cue 20	**Critic:** "... for the entire year." *Snap off spot on* **Critic** *and snap on spot on* **Naomi**	(Page 26)
Cue 21	**Naomi:** "... which means more money." *Snap on spot on* **Naomi** *and snap on spot on* **Daughter**	(Page 26)
Cue 22	**Daughter** "... that I could stand it." *Snap on spot on* **Critic**	(Page 26)
Cue 23	**Critic:** "... simply not cost effective." *Snap on spot on* **Naomi**	(Page 26)
Cue 24	**Naomi:** "... the preservation of life." *Snap on spot on* **Woman Critic**	(Page 26)
Cue 25	**Darbon** gives the thumbs-up sign *Snap off all spots*	(Page 26)
Cue 26	**Darbon** closes his eyes *Fade slowly in on* **Darbon**, *then to a Black-out*	(Page 29)

ACT II

To open: Full general lighting

Cue 27	The **Nurse** exits. A moment *Fade to lighting on* **Old Man**	(Page 40)
Cue 28	The **Old Man**'s eyes slowly close *Dim and start slow fade*	(Page 44)
Cue 29	The **Nurse** pulls back the curtains *Bring up general lighting*	(Page 44)
Cue 30	**Joan** gives advice on the telephone to **Barry** *Fade to Black-out*	(Page 56)

EFFECTS PLOT

ACT I

ACT II

MADE AND PRINTED IN GREAT BRITAIN BY
LATIMER TREND & COMPANY LTD PLYMOUTH